Whilst working on the text of this book, in addition to using our own information and arriving at our own conclusions, we drew upon the findings of research undertaken by the following historians:

Marie Bláhová, Petr Čornej, Zdeněk Dragoun, Tomáš Durdík, František Ekert, Michal Flegl, Jaroslav Herout, Ivan Hlaváček, Václav Hlavsa, Jaromír Homolka, Petr Chotěbor, Josef Janáček, František Kašička, Božena Kopičková, Dobroslav Líbal, Vilém Lorenc, Josef Mayer, Dobroslava Menclová, Bořivoj Nechvátal, Helena Olmerová, Emanuel Poche, Ctibor Rybár, Jiří Spěváček, Jaroslava Staňková, Karel Stejskal, František Šmahel, Jiří Štursa, Václav Vladivoj Tomek, Jiří Vančura, Milada Vilímková, Pavel Vlček, Svatopluk Voděra, Vojtěch Volavka, Zdeněk Wirth and Petr Wittlich.

PRAGUE

AN HISTORIC TOWN

MARIE VITOCHOVÁ

JINDŘICH KEJŘ

JIŘÍ VŠETEČKA

V RÁJI

No visitor to Prague can resist a look
at the painted calendar on Prague's
Astronomical Clock (orloj)

PRAGUE, MOTHER OF TOWNS

The Neo-Renaissance National Museum (Národní muzeum), erected in 1890 on a design by Josef Schulz, dominates Wenceslas Square (Václavské náměstí)

In the very heart of Bohemia (Čechy) lies Prague (Praha), capital of the Czech Republic, which for its beauty and sights has won the admiration of numerous visitors from around the world. The valley basin through which the river Vltava meanders was an enticing place in which to settle, since ancient trading routes passed through helpful fords in the river.

Thus, over hundreds of years, the future Czech capital grew on both the left and right banks of the river, out of small settlements which formed gradually in the area between two castles — the older Prague Castle (Pražský hrad), and Vyšehrad (higher castle), built later. Founded on sites overlooking the river in the 9th and 10th centuries, both castles marked the boundaries

of the area that was to become the Czech capital, and would, in the immediate future, influence fundamentally the expansion and structure of the settlement.

An old dynastic legend links the establishment of the town of Prague with the figure of Libuše, the fabled Czech princess and prophetess. When the princess summoned to her throne a ploughman from Stadice by the name of Přemysl, whom she chose to be her prince consort, she foretold the foundation of Prague with the words: "I see a large town, the glory of which shall reach the stars". That event, which occurred in pagan times, shortly after the Czech Slavs first came to inhabit the land, together with the cult of a later member of the Přemysl dynasty, Saint Wenceslas (died c. 935), became one of the foundations of mediaeval state and dynastic

9

tradition. In actual fact, the foundation of Prague Castle took place sometime after 880, when the first historically-attested Přemysl, Bořivoj, transferred the prince's residence here from Levý Hradec nad Vltavou, located nearby to the north. On a promontory above a bend in the river Vltava he erected a fortress and a church consecrated to Our Lady. Below the new stronghold, on the slopes and in the Vltava valley floor, villages and fishing communities were soon established, and a marketplace developed. The goods displayed here were both produced domestically and supplied by foreign traders, whose trading wagons often made their way along this route in order to take advantage of the fords. The traders stopped here under the protection of the prince's castle not only for commercial reasons, but also in order to rest a while before continuing on their journey.

The importance of Prague as the centre of a united country grew towards the end of the 10th century, when the Jewish trader, Ibrahim Ibn-Jacob, from Tortosa, in Iberia, visited Bohemia. The record of his travels, written in Arabic, is the first to depict Prague as an attractively built prince's residence, and gives an account of the extramural settlement, which was an important stop on long trade routes.

It is possible that by this time the second prince's castle, Vyšehrad, had already been built on a steep promontory on the southern edge of the Vltava river basin. Later tradition mistakenly referred to it as the predecessor to Prague Castle, although it is precisely the Vyšehrad rock which is connected with the legend of princess Libuše and her prophesies, said to have been uttered in that place high above the river.

In the course of the next two centuries still larger settlements with markets, which were often extensions of still older communities, sprang up in the area between the two castles. The importance, wealth and architectural beauty of these settlements — which, owing to their location, were then known by the name of Mezihradí (Between the Castles) — increased, and hence at this time the foundations were already being laid for the further urban expansion of the future Prague towns.

As the Romanesque period drew to a close, Prague was already a vast, urban-type settlement, comprising marketplaces, stone churches and the first monasteries, attractively built merchant houses, and farmsteads belonging to the landed gentry. A larger and more important settlement grew up on a broad and shallow part of the right bank of the basin. Communication with the prince's castle and with the settlements beneath it was provided firstly by a wooden, and subsequently by a stone, bridge. The process of transformation of the urban-type settlements on both banks of the Vltava into genuine towns culminated in the erection of ramparts. The ramparts were important not only because they served as a military defence, but also because they confirmed the consolidation of the unity of the municipal area, and created the preconditions within the ramparts for a peaceful and secure period in the life of the town.

The rapid expansion of Prague in the reign of the last of the Přemysl kings demonstrated the latter's growing authority within the realm, the increasing power of, and respect for the Czech state in central Europe, and of course the attention devoted to the development of royal towns, especially Prague. The castle became a magnificent royal residence, the nation's political centre and seat of power. Its requirements influenced Prague's economic growth as favourably as the increase in the population of the town, made possible by the settlement of undeveloped areas of the demarcated site. Another important factor in social and financial expansion amongst the town-dwellers was the discovery of rich silver deposits in Kutná Hora (mining mountain), Jihlava and Sezimovo Ústí. Its positive influence manifested itself in the political and economic growth of the entire kingdom, though, naturally, this source of wealth affected above all the development of Prague, the most important economic centre in the land.

Even internal power struggles in the early 1300s, which inflicted nothing but suffering and material losses upon Prague and many of its inhabitants, failed in the final analysis to weaken the economic growth of the town too dramatically or for any protracted length of time. The increase in the wealth of the inhabitants was manifested outwardly in the growth of everyday material culture. Changes were made above all to the dwellings of merchants and the more affluent craftsmen, although the practical spirit of the town-dwellers exerted only a slow influence on changes in construction trends. However, architectural trends were already absorbing fully a new Gothic style, which, admittedly, had been used much earlier and more impressively in the construction of sacred buildings. With the increase in wealth resulting from the healthy economic growth of the town, the bur-

Prague is breathtakingly beautiful at any time of the day or night. A number of places
afford a romantic view of Prague Castle (Pražský hrad). This is how it looks
from Novotny's Footbridge (Novotného lávka) at the Old Town Mills (Staroměstské mlýny)

11

ghers also began to harbour greater political ambitions. However, their aspirations were not realised until the reign of John of Luxemburg, when at last the monarch gave his consent to the establishment of a town hall as the seat of self-government for the town of Prague.

During its thousand-year evolution, Prague won many epithets extolling its beauty, architectural splendour and vastness. It was dubbed "Golden Prague" after the gilt roofs above the Prague Castle gates, and on another occasion "the town of a hundred spires" because of the innumerable towers and turrets of various shapes and the most diverse decoration rising above a sea of roofs belonging to Prague buildings. At this time Prague was already undergoing sweeping reconstruction and considerable enlargement in the reign of King Charles IV. He had decided to make the Prague settlements and both castles the stately capital not merely of the lands under the Czech crown, but also of the entire Holy Roman Empire, over which he was initially king, and later, emperor.

In the reign of Charles IV a new stone bridge was built across the Vltava, joining the greater, Old Town, with the smaller, Lesser Quarter (Malá Strana), lying beneath Prague Castle. On the Old Town side of the bridge a tall, impressive bridge tower was erected, adorned in Gothic style with stone sculptures of the monarch and his son Wenceslas, and with others of saints, coats of arms of the lands under the Czech crown and finely decorated Gothic motifs. Both dominant features of Prague in Charles' reign — the stone bridge and the Old Town Bridge Tower (Staroměstská mostecká věž) — were constructed by builders from Peter Parler's workshop. Charles also succeeded in making a reality his notion of enhancing the authority and renown of the royal seat through the foundation of a university. Not only would such an institution serve as a support for his political objectives and the practical aid supplied by the intellectual potential of learned scholars, but it would also attract students and masters from lands outside the realm. The university, established in 1348, soon became much-frequented, and subsequently was also a centre of intellectual religious opposition, receptive to the teachings of Wycliffe and other reformers. Prague in the reign of Charles IV also witnessed the work of Jan Milíč of Kroměříž, a town in Moravia. The intellectual polemics and declaimers arising out of his discussions with religious contemporaries were a portent of widespread uprisings in the kingdom of Bohemia.

During Charles' reign the Dutchman Geert Groote, son of the burgomaster in Deventer and a canon in Utrecht and Aix-la-Chapelle, arrived in Prague at a time when the town was rapidly expanding and accruing wealth, thanks to the prosperity secured by the standing of Charles IV, King of Bohemia and Holy Roman Emperor. It was his membership of a town hall mission and the reputation enjoyed by Prague University that brought him to Prague from Deventer, since as a master of liberal arts from Paris University he would have undoubtedly expressed an interest in participating in a delegation to the town. Jan Milíč of Kroměříž, whom Groote certainly met, greatly influenced his later life. Eventually he also decided to live in obedience to God's law, modestly and in chastity, as Jan Milíč of Kroměříž was striving to do in Prague. Thus, thanks to the Dutchman Groote, the teachings of the forerunner of the great Czech reformers spread to that distant country by the sea. Groote himself fell into disfavour in his homeland for disseminating "heresy", but his followers continued to spread his ideas, even when persecuted for it by the Inquisition. In Prague, Milíč's work was continued by Konrad Waldhauser, and later by Friedrich Eppinge, Nicholas and Peter of Dresden, Jan Hus (John Huss), Jerome of Prague and other reformers.

The greatest changes were made to Prague in the reign of Charles IV through the foundation of a new town outside the Old Town walls. The monarch took other large European cities as his model in expanding the original boundaries of Prague on the banks of the Vltava into the New Town, which he enclosed within walls with numerous towers and gates. In addition, he greatly enlarged the delimited area of the Lesser Quarter with new ramparts extending from the Strahov Monastery (Strahovský klášter) over Petřín Hill and down as far as the river. Vyšehrad, the second royal castle in Prague, was constructed anew and given modern fortifications, the aim being to make it a residence as fit for a sovereign as the chief castle of the realm, Prague Castle. In this way Charles IV laid the foundations of the city, the area of which, enclosed within new fortifications, was only partly and gradually built upon until the 19th century.

Following Charles' death his son, Wenceslas IV, was deposed from the throne of Rome, and as a consequence Prague quickly lost its importance as the seat

The Golden Lane (Zlatá ulička) at Prague Castle is perhaps the place most sought after by visitors to Prague. The small houses with their multi-coloured façades are built into the castle wall above Stag Moat (Jelení příkop)

13

The historic Old Town Hall complex (Staroměstská radnice) with its massive, prismatic Gothic tower dating from the mid-14th century and its famous Astronomical Clock (orloj)

14

The splendid Renaissance House At the Minute (dům U Minuty), with its extraordinary
façade decorated with *sgraffito* figures and floral motifs, fits in well
amongst the historic Old Town Hall buildings

15

of the most powerful ruler in Christendom at that time. Nevertheless, in the historic period that ensued, namely the Hussite Revolution — the prelude to the great European revolutions — the inhabitants of Prague themselves and their political representatives took perfect advantage of the town's economic and military potential from the very outset of the revolution and, with the help of their provincial allies, played a rôle far beyond the frontiers of the Bohemian kingdom. The chalice came to represent more than a mere emblem of the victorious revolution, becoming rather the very result, since it was even recognised by the Council, then the highest body in the Church. At that time Prague was the true centre of the Czech lands and the acknowledged heart of Hussite Bohemia, something that was respected by both its local allies and by its foreign and domestic enemies.

Even finding itself without a sovereign towards the mid-15th century, Prague retained its status, and the council room in the Old Town Hall emerged as the place where the fate of the entire nation was often decided. Hence it was no accident that the high political prestige of Prague's inhabitants was further confirmed at the town hall by the choice of a new Czech king from amongst the country's nobles. George of Poděbrady (Jiří z Poděbrad) ascended the royal throne to become the ruler over two peoples — Catholics and Utraquists.

George of Poděbrady, famous *inter alia* for the peacemaking efforts he directed towards the rulers of Christendom, was succeeded by monarchs from the Polish Jagellon dynasty. During their reign the image of Gothic Prague and its castle was completed, enriched by real treasures of late Gothic architecture. Nevertheless, during the same period Prague lost its status as the royal seat when Vladislav II of Jagellon, after ascending also the Hungarian throne, transferred the royal residence to Buda, as he had earlier pledged to do to the Hungarian Estates during the electoral process. In the internecine political struggles with the aristocracy, Prague, as the head of the royal towns, was a consistent advocate of the validity of its third vote in the Estates-General. In 1508 that third vote was also conferred upon the towns, and in 1517 the disputes between the nobles and knights on the one hand, and the federation of towns — represented notably by Prague — on the other, were settled by the so-called Treaty of Saint Wenceslas. This important document, though far from able to resolve all causes of tension in the mutual relations between the opposing parties, served in part to guarantee the political and economic status that Prague and other royal towns had previously acquired. However, when the citizens of Prague participated in the first, disastrous uprising by the Estates against Ferdinand I in 1547, the victorious monarch was able to subjugate fully a city which, on account of its political authority and economic power, had for many decades been accustomed to behaving in a manner somewhat detached from the remainder of the realm. With the establishment of the institution of the king's magistrates and provosts, municipal self-government came to depend entirely upon those officials appointed by the king from amongst the aristocracy. Thus the political head of the municipal Estate — Prague's Old Town Hall — became a subordinate institution with no real possibility of pursuing an independent policy.

At the close of the 16th century, whilst Rudolf II was on the throne, Prague regained its former splendour as a royal seat, for the Emperor, in whose reign the Renaissance period of Prague's restoration was brought to completion, was an admirer and patron of the arts. And so it was that at his court in Prague, alongside the political personalities sent there from royal courts throughout Europe, there appeared also painters, sculptors, musicians, men of letters, astrologers and even alchemists from all parts, for the erudite Emperor took an interest in everyone, and each received material support.

However, by that time Bohemia was already moving gradually towards a conflict between the authorities and the Church which, despite its having been averted a number of times by diplomatic activity on both sides, finally erupted in 1618. Its consequences reached far beyond Prague and Bohemia; in fact, this conflict between Catholics and Protestants plunged the whole of Europe into the Thirty Years' War. The dangerous flames of that fire were lit in Prague on 23 May 1618, when the Protestant Estates threw Catholic royal councillors out of the windows of the so-called Ludvik Wing (Ludvíkovo křídlo) of the Royal Palace (Královský palác) in Prague Castle — an act known as defenestration — and thus gave the signal for the second uprising by the Estates to commence. It is interesting to note that public reaction

16

A detail from a stained-glass window in the Archbishop's Chapel (Arcibiskupská kaple) in St. Vitus' Cathedral (katedrála svatého Víta) at Prague Castle. It was copied from a model by Alfons Mucha, and is an example of his later Art Nouveau work

17

Úvoz, a street in castle district of Hradčany, offers the visitor to Prague many views of the town.
This vista of greenery shows the roofs of the Lesser Quarter and the tower and
dome of the Church of St. Nicholas (kostel sv. Mikuláše)

18

in the Netherlands to the Czech Estates' uprising was highly favourable. The Dutch States-General were particularly conscious of the importance of the conflict with the Habsburgs, and they were pleased by the Czechs' resistance to Vienna. But that was not all. There followed both diplomatic and military support, with the Dutch States-General financing the dispatch of military reinforcements to Bohemia. However, the entire anti-Habsburg revolt by Czech Protestants came to an inglorious end two years later with their defeat at the hands of the troops of the Emperor and the Catholic League at the Battle of White Mountain (Bílá hora). There followed the hasty escape by Frederick of the Palatinate, dubbed the "Winter King" because his rule over Bohemia lasted only one winter; executions of the rebel Estates' leaders, including representatives of the Prague towns, on the Old Town Square; the forced re-catholicisation of the majority of citizens; and the first great Bohemian and Moravian exodus, which included such great figures as Comenius (Jan Amos Komenský).

Many Prague citizens were fined for participating — albeit for the most part passively — in the revolt, and thousands of people preferred to leave the country rather than renounce their faith. However, the severest consequence for Prague of the disaster at White Mountain was economic and political decay. Thereafter the Czech capital became little more than a provincial town within the Habsburg Empire, and the devastating Thirty Years' War, which affected Prague directly on several occasions, simply accelerated the political and economic decline of the town.

In apparent contradiction with the aforementioned developments, building activity was recommenced rapidly in the aftermath of the Thirty Years' War. The reason for this was the need to refortify solidly Prague and its castles, as the unfortunate experiences of the recent war had shown, though this time fully in keeping with the Baroque style of building fortifica-

The Castle gardens are remarkable for their garden architecture. One of the best examples is the Royal Garden (Královská zahrada), with its wealth of sculptures and statues, some of which are from the studio of the leading Baroque sculptor Matthias Bernard Braun

19

The Church of St. Nicholas in the Lesser Quarter is perhaps the most distinctive
of Prague Baroque structures. The huge statues of religious teachers
inside the Church are the work of sculptor Ignaz Platzer

The richly decorated main door leading into the chapter Church of SS Peter
and Paul (kostel sv. Petra a Pavla) at Vyšehrad. The crossed
keys are the symbol of the Vyšehrad chapter

This view of the Lesser Quarter also highlights the sheer size of the Church of
St. Nicholas. Rising up between its dome and tower is the narrow
tower of the Church of St. Thomas (kostel sv. Tomáše)

tions. Renewed construction was also aided by the large-scale confiscation of property belonging to non-Catholics, which served as the areal and financial basis for the erection of large church buildings and new houses for those aristocratic families on the winning side at White Mountain. Soon after the end of the Thirty Years' War Baroque architecture began to take a hold in Prague — which in spite of its Renaissance veneer had retained its mediaeval character — and transform it into a Baroque town with stunning and imposing architecture on both sides of the river Vltava. The substantial change which Baroque architecture brought to Prague had a certain unifying effect, in that it gave the town a new, uniform appearance. New palaces were built and ornamental gardens designed, and the latest trends in the building of fortifications were employed in the New Town, the Lesser Quarter, Vyšehrad, Prague Castle and Hradčany. Churches, monasteries, hospitals and houses for the town burghers — including properties outside the city walls — some of which have survived to this day, were constructed or reconstructed. Substantial remodelling was carried out on both Prague castles; whilst Vyšehrad steadily took on the appearance of an imposing Baroque fortress to defend the town from the south in order to fulfil the aims of the state, Prague Castle underwent reconstruction work on a grandiose scale, which reached its height in the Neoclassical period, during the reign of Maria Theresa.

The Rococo and Neoclassical styles completed the transformation of mediaeval Prague. The greater part of building activities was rechannelled into orders for the nouveaux riches of the town, which formed the

The Waldstein Palace and Palace Gardens (Valdštejnský palác a palácová zahrada). The imposing sala terrena was completed in 1627 on the basis of a design by architect Giovanni Pieroni. The Waldstein Gardens afford a magnificent view of Prague Castle

23

A detail from the decoration on the façade of Prague's Municipal House (Obecní dům), an extraordinary building dating from the early 20th century. The balustrade, with its Art Nouveau ornamentation, is dominated by the Prague town coat of arms

This example of Prague Art Nouveau is taken from the decoration on the façade of the building erected for the former Prague Insurance Company by Oswald Polívka. The relief is the work of sculptor Ladislav Šaloun

24

basis for the transformation of Prague into a picturesque and peaceful place. The Baroque domes and onion domes, mansard roofs, gables and dormer windows, the Rococo and Neoclassical façades on the buildings in the town below, and rising up above them the Neoclassical palace façades at Prague Castle, endowed Prague and its panorama with an entirely new character.

However, the mediaeval way of town life was preserved within its walls almost until the end of the 18th century. No great upheaval took place before the economic and social changes effected in the reign of Joseph II. In 1784 the towns of Prague — the Old Town, the New Town, the Lesser Quarter and Hradčany — were brought together as a single entity with a joint municipal council. In implementing his reformist policy, the enlightened Emperor did not overlook the Prague ghetto, and in his decree abolished its isolation, dating back to the Middle Ages. Nonetheless, the Jewish Quarter, subsequently renamed Josefov (Joseph Quarter), did not receive full emancipation until 1850, when it was proclaimed the fifth district of Prague. In 1883 a sixth district, Vyšehrad, was added, and in the years that followed the Prague agglomeration spread at lightning speed.

The Austro-Prussian war of 1866 demonstrated that the vast Baroque fortifications, which essentially followed the course of the mediaeval ramparts of the Old Town and the Lesser Quarter, were ineffective from the military point of view, and moreover hampered the economic and architectural expansion of Prague. However, it was not until after 1871 that the town walls were demolished. In spite of this, beyond the fortifications, the first industrial companies had been springing up since the 1830s, the population increased, and former villages became densely populated towns practically overnight. Industrial expansion was also nurtured by the introduction of rail transport, local public transport, horse-drawn trams and, by the close of the century, even electric trams. 19th-century Prague witnessed the construction of a whole series of new public buildings and new streets with the houses of the middle class imitating architectural styles. To the Neo-Gothic, Neo-Renaissance and Neoclassical styles visible on the streets of Prague were added Neo-Baroque and, more especially, in the early 20th century, Art Nouveau architecture. Moreover, at this time new areas of the town were already being constructed in accordance with modern architectural criteria.

In 1918 Prague became the capital of the Czechoslovak state, and under a law passed two years later, Greater Prague came into existence, incorporating large suburbs which until then had enjoyed the status of independent towns, as well as dozens of villages and communities covering a vast area. The interwar period saw a dramatic population increase, leading in turn to a building boom. New residential areas and industrial complexes were created on the outskirts of the city, and the construction of family houses in the suburbs increased. The entrepreneurial spirit linked to the architectural avant-garde reached the very heart of the city. The results were not always the happiest, but in a number of cases the achievements were remarkable and of major cultural importance.

Prague continued to grow even after the interruption of the Second World War and the Nazi occupation, its area being enlarged a further three times. In spite of a whole series of difficulties caused by the inadequate care devoted to certain vitally important services, and by the insufficient community facilities in new residential areas and their austere nature and transport difficulties, Prague is now ready to solve its ecological and transport problems and insufficiencies in the maintenance of the city proper and in the structure of the tertiary sector. A great deal of effort, and above all considerable financial resources, will be required in restoring Prague's historic nucleus, a large part of which has been classified as being of particular historic value. Moreover, the Prague Castle grounds constitute a special area from the point of view of historic monuments, and in the same way a number of other prominent structures enjoy the highest degree of protection as national cultural monuments.

The Prague of today is a city in a free country, the capital of the Czech Republic. It is an open book of the events that have occurred in a nation and on a continent, and generously offers its beauty, cultural treasures and historical testimony to those who wish to see them.

The entire northern side of the Old Town Square is dominated by the Church consecrated to St. Nicholas, an impressive building from the Prague Baroque period, constructed between 1732 and 1735 on a design by Kilian Ignaz Dientzenhofer

The visitor enters the Prague Castle grounds through the so-called Matthias Gate (1614).
This rare early Baroque structure is thought to have been
designed by Italian architect Vicenzo Scamozzi

PRAGUE CASTLE

Prague Castle is the seat of the President of the Czech Republic. Hundreds of onlookers watch the regular ceremony of the changing of the Castle guard, which is also attended by the Castle's military band in its red uniform

From this castle shall sprout two golden olive trees, whose crowns shall reach the seventh heaven, and they shall sparkle throughout the world with signs and miracles. All the tribes of Bohemia and other peoples shall honour them with offerings and gifts. One of them shall be called Maior gloria (Greater Glory), and the other Exercitus consolatio (Consolation to soldiers). This shall come to pass in the distant future. For the lives of the glorious prince of the Kingdom of Bohemia, the celebrated martyr Wenceslas, who in Slavonic is called Václav, which is translated as Magna gloria (Great Glory), and of Adalbert the Blessed, martyr and second bishop of Prague, whose Slavonic name, Vojtěch, is translated as Consolatio exercitus (Consolation to soldiers), blossomed in the said castle.

FROM THE PROPHECY BY PRINCESS LIBUŠE IN THE CHRONICLE OF BOHEMIA
BY PŘIBÍK OF RADENÍN, CALLED PULKAVA

29

The prince's stronghold, later the castle of the kings of Bohemia, was founded on the headland which opens wide to the south in the Vltava basin, and which to the north is separated by a high valley through which the Brusnice stream flows on its way downstream to join the Vltava. The long shape of the headland sloping down to the river on the eastern side reminded the Czechs of the period of the long spine and tail of a dog, or of the body of a dolphin, hence the mention made of this comparison even in the oldest records. On the western, most accessible side, cutting across the path to the fortress was a broad moat spanned by a bridge which, as mentioned by the earliest Czech chronicler, Cosmas, dates back to 1004.

The original pre-Romanesque stronghold was probably founded some time after 880 by Prince Bořivoj who earlier, together with his consort Ludmila, had been baptised by the Slavonic apostle Methodius. It was in these parts that Bořivoj subsequently also founded the first Christian church, consecrated to Our Lady; the remains of the church's foundations have been preserved to this day.

In the middle of the fortress stood a covered court, to the east of which, some time before 920, Prince Vratislav I founded the little Church of St. George (sv. Jiří), later reconstructed as a Romanesque basilica with a Benedictine convent. On the western side, likewise on the axis of the castle site, Vratislav's son Wenceslas had a two-level stone rotunda erected. It was consecrated to Saint Vitus (sv. Vít) after 929, and was to become the most important cathedral in Bohemia. After the establishment of an independent bishopric in 973 (the first bishop was the Saxon Dietmar), a Bishop's chapel was also built and consecrated to St. Maurice.

The personage of Prince Wenceslas is significant as regards both Prague Castle and, of course, the history of the entire Czech nation, since he became the country's first saint and is its patron saint. However, Wenceslas was murdered in 935 in a conspiracy involving magnates at the castle of his younger brother Boleslav, who had been privy to the preparations for the coup d'état and the assassination. On the one hand legends depict Boleslav I as a fratricide, whilst on the other they underline the care he took over the burial of the prince's remains in St. Vitus' Rotunda, chosen by Wenceslas himself as his final resting place. Boleslav succeeded Saint Wenceslas as prince, and in his reign the power of the Bohemian state increased rapidly, in spite of a persistent threat from the empire ruled by Otto I. The Christianisation of the country continued, and Boleslav's endeavours to strengthen the authority of the Church culminated during the reign of his son, Boleslav II, in the establishment of a bishopric for Bohemia, albeit subordinate to the archbishopric in Mainz. It was not long before Prince Wenceslas was being fêted as a saint and peacemaker, and later as the patron saint of the nation and the mystical keeper of Bohemian monarchical power, conferred upon living members of the House of Přemysl and their successors alone. All that remain of Wenceslas' rotunda are parts of the masonry, especially those from the southern apse with the saint's tomb, now located in St. Wenceslas' Chapel in the Cathedral, into which Wenceslas' original little church was transformed over the centuries.

In approximately 1050 Prince Břetislav I ordered the replacement of the castle ramparts with stone walls, and in 1060, on the site where Wenceslas' rotunda stood, Prince Spytihněv II commenced work on a basilica consecrated to the martyred saints Vitus, Wenceslas and Adalbert, with two chancels, the west chancel being consecrated to Our Lady. The construction work even survived a castle fire, and was completed during the reign of the first King of Bohemia, Vratislav, in about 1090. At that time a monastery for the Church in Prague was erected, and was home to the metropolitan chapter, founded before the end of the millenium. The chapter played a significant rôle in culture and education — its school of latin was the highest centre of education until the university was founded — and also in the development of the state, which quite simply could not manage without the administrative and diplomatic activities of the learned men of the Church. However, it was King Vratislav I himself who thus attempted to counterbalance the excessive influence exerted by the St. Vitus canons through the establishment of a new chapter at Vyšehrad. We are also obliged to the St. Vitus chapter for the oldest preserved chronicle of Bohemia, written by the erudite and much-travelled Cosmas (d. 1125). Throughout his long life he recorded ancient stories and legends and authentic testimonies of the events which occurred in the country and in Europe.

Dating from the early 16th century, the so-called Ludvik Wing (Ludvíkovo křídlo)
of the Royal Palace (Královský palác) in Prague Castle is an example
of pure Renaissance style. Its author was Benedict Ried of Pístov

31

The 12th century was a turbulent one for Prague Castle, and yet the abrupt changes wrought by successive monarchs and wars failed to halt the growth of the nation, the settlement beneath the castle, and the residence of the sovereign, the castle itself. After 1135, Prince Soběslav I commenced reconstruction on the castle in "metropolis Bohemiae Pragam more Latinorum civitatum colpit renovari": that is to say, he began to restore the principal castle in Bohemia using the methods employed in Romanesque cities to the west and south of the country's wooded borders. The entire castle ramparts were meticulously lined with white ashlar veneer and fortified, as is still discernable in the interior and on the façades of later castle buildings, particular on the south and west sides. The prince's palace at the southern end of the castle was reconstructed into a large, representative palace with three towers and a two-level All Saints' Chapel. The Bishop of Prague's residence was also restored; a fragment of it can still be seen today in the façade of the old provost's residence in the third castle courtyard. After the castle was besieged by Conrad of Znojmo in 1142, and set on fire by a "flaming arrow", St. George's Basilica and Benedictine convent were renovated. Ever since the prince's sister, Mlada, had founded the convent, the abbess had been a member of the ruling house with the title of princess-abbess, and held the right to crown the Queen of Bohemia. The convent emerged as a prestigious educational institution for ladies of noble birth, and made a significant contribution to the growth of spiritual and material culture alike in the Bohemia of the Middle Ages.

In the 13th century the mediaeval Bohemian state expanded further. Přemysl Otakar I succeeded in obtaining the diplomatic recognition of Bohemia's sovereignty and of the royal succession. His endeavours were crowned to this effect in 1212 when Frederic II issued a document known as the Golden Bull of Sicily, because of the way in which it was sealed. In the reign of King Wenceslas I Prague Castle was witness to a power struggle between the monarch and his son, Přemysl Otakar.

During the economic upsurge, the Přemysls concentrated their efforts on creating new towns in the country and erecting castles. Prague Castle was also extended further westwards through the establishment of a large settlement, its fortifications were improved, and a walkway with arcades and nine Gothic pointed arches was added to the upper level of the original Romanesque palace. A chapel consecrated to All Saints was also adjoined to the palace.

Following the fateful battle against the army of Rudolf of Habsburg in Moravia, at which Přemysl Otakar II was defeated, and the ensuing disintegration of the kingdom, it was his son, Wenceslas II, who first managed to grasp firmly the reins of monarchical power. By means of a prudent domestic policy — which, although often characterised by intrigue, was also marked by great skill on the part of his advisors — he gradually eliminated his foreign enemies on the diplomatic scene and led the country to renewed prosperity. He was also crowned king of Poland, and despite the fact that the Hungarian throne was offered to him as well, it was his son, Wenceslas III, who finally accepted it. Thus, Prague Castle came to be the seat of a powerful ruler who aimed to win the ultimate prize in Christendom at that time. It was only the premature death of a king of Bohemia whose health had always been fragile which prevented him from obtaining the glittering prize of the crown of the Roman Empire.

The architectural richness of Prague Castle and the town itself, as well as the increasing power of the Bohemian crown, were influenced to a great degree by silver. The metal was mined in many places in Bohemia at the time, above all in Kutná Hora, and as a consequence the town came to rank behind Prague (Old Town) alone in terms of wealth and size. In 1300 coins made from Czech silver — known as the Prague groš, or penny — were struck for the first time, and became a much sought after currency outside the country as well. On the death of Wenceslas II in 1305 his young son, Wenceslas III, not yet seventeen years of age, assumed the throne. His reign was short, as he was murdered a year later by a hired assassin in the Moravian town of Olomouc, where the king's troops had gathered for a campaign in Poland.

There followed the short reigns of Rudolf of Austria and Henry of Carinthia, after which John of Luxemburg, son of Henry VII, Count of Luxemburg and Roman King and Emperor, succeeded to the throne of Bohemia, taking as his consort Elizabeth Přemysl, the last unmarried Přemysl princess. The young John entered Bohemia with his army in 1310, and after a short

The Neo-Gothic façade of St. Vitus' Cathedral and its towers date from
the time of completion of the building in the latter half
of the 19th century and early 20th century

33

The sober, graceful lines of St. Vitus' Cathedral at Prague Castle
are complemented in an interior adorned with the more lavish
forms of Baroque statues of saints

A detail from the chancel in St. Vitus' Cathedral. The stained-glass windows, produced according to a design by Max Švabinský, depict the Holy Trinity, with Our Lady and Prince Spytihněv on the left, and Saint Wenceslas and Charles IV on the right

St. Vitus' Cathedral is the nation's most important cathedral. Work on the structure, begun by builders Matthew of Arras and Peter Parler in the 14th century, was not completed until the beginning of the 20th century

St. Vitus' Cathedral (katedrála sv. Víta) also houses the bodily remains
of the Czech saint John Nepomuk, canonised in 1729.
The tomb was built between 1733 and 1736

campaign against supporters of the deposed Henry of Carinthia, on 6 December he marched victoriously into Prague, by now under the control of his and Elizabeth's supporters. On 7 February 1311 the king and his consort were crowned by the Bishop of Mainz, Peter of Aspelt, in St. Vitus' Basilica at Prague Castle. However, the coronation banquet had to be held in the Franciscan monastery of St. James, since the castle remained uninhabitable as the result of a fire in 1303 and its recent disastrous occupation by troops from Meissen, invited there by the former King Henry of Carinthia to protect him.

I t is no easy matter to describe the personage of John of Luxemburg in brief. Famed as a diplomat, warrior and entrepreneur, he embodied the chivalrous virtues of the era. He was an example of elegance; the Christian world admired his courage, and deliberation and impulsiveness were both evident in his demeanour. Although he cared little for the management of domestic affairs (unless he urgently needed further, non-repayable loans from his subjects), he bore the Bohemian royal coat of arms proudly at every royal court, in every tournament arena, and on every battlefield in Europe — until 26 August 1346, when, now blind, he entered into battle between two of his pages' horses, as he had commanded, and was brought down, sword in hand, amongst French knights at the Battle of Crécy against the English.

John's son Charles was elected King of Rome, and in accordance with the former's last will and testament, written in 1340, and in the light of a decision by the Estates-General of Bohemia and of the acts of homage paid by Prague and the princes of Silesia in 1341, he also ascended the Bohemian throne. Having already ruled Bohemia for thirteen years for his father, who had been absent almost permanently, Charles was, therefore, well-versed in such matters. At the age of seven he had been taken by his father to the French royal court, and had been looked after by Queen Marie. The official reason for sending him there was for him to receive his education, but underlying this were John's fears that the Bohemian noblesse might dethrone him in favour of his son, still a minor. Nonetheless, Charles' hard journey through life was to prove nothing but an asset to his future and to the Czech lands. The perfect education, extraordinary po-

litical insight, artful diplomacy and cultural ambitions were precisely what the next ruler of Bohemia required. He was educated by Roger des Rosiers from Limoges, abbot at Fécamp and subsequently Pope Clement VI, "an eloquent and erudite man, graced with the manners of great nobility". The spiritual ambiance of the Sorbonne, and the influence of legal theory and practice as embraced by legists at the French court, produced a favourable effect upon the prince.

In the final two years before Charles' return to his homeland, his father allowed him a taste of a monarch's duties — first of all in the Duchy of Luxemburg, and later in the hotbed of the seigneurie of Luxemburg in northern Italy, where he represented his father for some time and displayed his courage and chivalry to the full. We have dwelt somewhat at length on Charles' childhood in order to make it clear as to why, upon returning to his native land at such a young age, it was possible for him to show himself so evidently to be a level-headed and energetic ruler, a cultured and clear-minded person, and a sovereign who achieved practically everything he set out to do.

Charles took decisive measures to clear crown property of its debts and, more gradually, its prepaid pledges. He began the restoration of Prague Castle in the style of the seat of the French monarchs, beginning first of all with the complete rebuilding of the Royal Palace. In this he proceeded decisively but prudently, trying to blend new features and architectural elements with an accent on tradition and the *genius loci*. The new palace respected fully the older, valuable sections of the building, namely the Romanesque substructure and the preserved areas of Přemysl Otakar II's palace. The central room was the Great Hall, linked via a bridge to the adjacent All Saints' Chapel — the *mirabile opere*. The Sainte-Chapelle in Paris undoubtedly served as the model for this noble structure, which comprises a rich, round frame filled with colourful stained-glass windows.

Charles used every available means in his attempt to strengthen the rule of law and the country's standing abroad. An expression of his determination as monarch was the crowning of the efforts made by the House of Přemysl for centuries to free the country from subordination to the archbishopric of Mainz. Even prior to his father's death he had succeeded in obtaining the issuance of the relevant bull from Clement VI, and in 1344 the educated Ernest of Par-

The early Baroque façade of the Church of St. George (kostel sv. Jiří) conceals
from the visitor the original three-aisle Romanesque Basilica
with its two distinctive white towers

The most attractive part of Prague Castle is the Golden Lane. During the reign
of Rudolf II, the tiny cottages housed the Castle marksmen
and goldsmiths

dubice, who later became Charles' chancellor and invaluable counsellor, was appointed the first metropolitan of Prague. In that same year the foundations were laid of the new cathedral of St. Vitus. Construction work on the structure was begun by master builder Matthew of Arras. Here also, Charles took an innovative approach, whilst respecting tradition. The new building work did not change the sequence of chapels or the consecration of the altars, above all the Chapel of St. Wenceslas, which became the nation's ideological centre. Charles understood from personal experience during his stay at the French royal court the deep significance attached to the coronation of the monarch and the symbolism of the ceremony. The crown of the kings of Bohemia was consecrated to its princely patron saint, despite the fact that Charles had it substantially remodelled, embellishing it with new precious stones and relics, and also secured its legal protection and status, on the one hand through the issuance of a Code for the Coronation of the Kings of Bohemia, and on the other through a regulation by the supreme authority of the Church, Pope Clement VI, who granted his protégé a papal bull to the same effect.

Thanks to Charles, Prague Castle became the residence of the king of Rome, and later of the Holy Roman Emperor. It witnessed the hustle and bustle of diplomatic activity and royal visits, in much the same way as the newly-built Emperor's castle at Karlštejn, situated not far from Prague on the way to Nuremberg. The team of artists employed by Charles, including such people as the multi-talented Peter Parler, master of St. Vitus' workshop, or master painters Theodore and Nicholas Wurmser, worked on numerous construction projects not only in Prague itself, but also throughout Bohemia and in other countries. The decorative arts flourished, one example being that of Prague goldsmiths, who took both their designs and their competitive stimulus from the works which Charles brought with him from abroad. When Charles IV died in 1378, he left behind the active seeds of an developing residence. However, the circumstances changed completely in the reign of his son Wenceslas IV. Construction and decorative work continued — albeit at a basically slower rate — but the king himself moved into the royal court in the Old Town, which became the royal residence for the next hundred years.

During the early stages of the Hussite Revolution the Castle housed a strong garrison loyal to Sigismund, King of Hungary and Rome, whom the Hussites had refused to recognise, and who thus constituted a permanent threat to Utraquist Prague. For this reason, the Hussites laid siege to the castle in the spring of 1421, occupying not only a considerable part of Hradčany, but also the vineyards beneath the castle. As soon as the garrison, despairing of the situation, surrendered, the Hussites took the castle.

The sweeping reconstruction work carried out on Prague Castle in the reign of the House of Jagellon is linked first and foremost with the name of Benedict Ried of Pístov. He probably began by rebuilding the castle fortifications, rendered necessary by the development in ordnance techniques. The first priority was to strengthen the defences at both gates: an advanced fortification was built at the west gate, and at the east gate a barbican was erected. Several artillery towers — the most famous being the Daliborka tower, which also served as a prison — completed the overall fortification system. However, Ried's mastery left a lasting impression above all in the revamping of the Royal Palace, the Vladislav Audience Chamber (Vladislavova audienční síň) and the Vladislav Hall (Vladislavský sál), undertaken between 1490 and 1502, the most important monuments to Ried's work. The arched vaults create a startling impression, and equally admirable is the so-called Riders' Staircase (Jezdecké schody), that is to say the main ceremonial flight of steps leading into the Vladislav Hall. The restoration of the Royal Palace's west wing, and the new royal oratory in St. Vitus' Cathedral, are without doubt the work of Hans Spiess from Frankfurt. Subsequently, between 1503 and 1510, Ried erected the so-called Ludvik Wing of the palace in pure Renaissance style. The façade of the building facing towards the towns is dotted with early Renaissance windows.

King Ludvik of Jagellon died tragically whilst fleeing the Turks following his defeat at the Battle of Mohács in Hungary, and thus Bohemia found herself faced with the election a new king, from which Archduke Ferdinand of Austria, brother-in-law of Ludvik and brother of Emperor Charles V, emerged the victor. It is surprising that the self-confident, overwhelmingly non-Catholic Estates-General chose as their king a devout Catholic and, moreover, an advocate of strong, centralised rule. Although Ferdinand signed the electo-

41

ral declaration in which he undertook to respect both common and codified law, he had already resolved to comply with them as little as possible, in order to build a strong central European Habsburg monarchy. Attempts at re-catholicisation, the political restrictions imposed upon town Estates, and efforts at centralisation represented the negative side of Ferdinand's reign, which continued until the 1560s, by which time he had already succeeded his brother as Emperor. In spite of this, the care devoted to Prague Castle constitutes one of the more positive aspects of his rule.

So the mediaeval castle of old was gradually changed into a Renaissance residence, some of the most beautiful examples of this style being the east and west windows of Vladislav's palace. Ferdinand began by constructing new royal rooms west of the original Royal Palace, and beyond Stag Moat he created the Royal Garden with the Royal Summer, or Belvedere, Palace (Královský letohrádek); the latter was designed by the Italian architect Paolo della Stella, and erected by Bonifaz Wohlmut. The Royal Garden, which postdates 1534, is the purest expression of the import of the Italian Renaissance north of the Alps; the landscaping of the garden was modelled on the gardens of Italy. The real jewel in the crown is the Singing Fountain, erected between 1564 and 1568, so named after the sound of the drops of water falling into the bell-metal basin.

The implementation of the Renaissance project for Prague Castle was held up for a time when fire engulfed the entire left-bank area of Prague, including the castle itself, on 2 June 1541. By then Ferdinand was fully engaged by his brother, Emperor Charles, in affairs relating to the Empire. In August 1547, Ferdinand I showed unprecedented cruelty in dealing with the first anti-Habsburg revolt at the so-called "St. Bartholomew massacre"; the castle was witness to these humiliating moments for the people of Prague. Ferdinand left his son and namesake, the future Archduke of the Tirol, in the town as his representative. Together with his consort, Philippina Welser, the younger Ferdinand kept a Renaissance court whose links with the Czech environment were closer, and whilst he resided at the castle his convictions contributed to the growth of the Renaissance and of humanist thinking.

The construction of a Renaissance seat at Prague Castle, which in the wake of the fire took place together with the erection of palaces for the noblesse — the Burgrave's Palace, or Rožmberk and Lobkowicz Palaces, for instance — continued under Ferdinand's successor, Maximilian II, and was concluded by Rudolf II. In the course of Rudolf's reign, spanning almost three decades, the emperor once again took Prague Castle as his residence, a resurgence in trade occurred, and the arts and crafts flourished. The well-educated and cultured sovereign was tormented both physically and mentally by a serious, protracted illness, and as a consequence he became more and more introvert; yet this did nothing to dampen his enthusiasm for the construction and decoration of new buildings or the landscaping of gardens, nor his collecting mania. In Rudolf II's time, the Renaissance chapter in the castle's life came to a close, and made way for the Mannerist period. Beneath Rudolph's new, long palace, on the southern side facing the town, a Paradise Garden was planted to replace the old vineyards (the garden as seen today having been landscaped after 1920 by Josip Plečnik). Alongside the reconstruction of All Saints' Chapel and the decoration of St. Vitus' Cathedral, between 1584 and 1606 the emperor ordered the building of a new north palace with two large halls, a shorter wing opposite St. Vitus' Cathedral with a mathematical tower, and next to it a new Spanish Hall (Španělský sál), designed by the emperor's architect, Giovanni Maria Filippi. The Golden Lane we see today, with its little houses built tightly into the castle wall, dates back to this period as well. Rudolf's court was one of the foremost centres of European Mannerism, the importance of which has only recently come to be appreciated. Prague became a focal point for artists, scholars, and notably astronomers, astrologers and alchemists, and for the art market, dominated by the emperor's passion for art. His need to collect works of art, products of nature, rare artefacts and antique finds, was satisfied by dozens of agents. The emperor was indeed a generous patron of science and art, and was thus surrounded not only by scientists and artists, but also by various charlatans and crooks. At the same time also, Prague became host to a sizeable community of Italian artists, woodcarvers, stonemasons, builders and plasterers, and still more arrived from the Rhineland and the Netherlands.

This section of the original northern defences of Prague Castle above Stag Moat
(Jelení příkop) is an example of late
Gothic fortifications

43

A good many families who arrived at that time made their homes here permanently.

Beyond the castle walls which protected the emperor's tranquility, conflicts — namely the continuing Turkish expansion, and above all the European religious crisis, which also shook the kingdom of Bohemia — were persistently making their presence felt. The majority of non-Catholic Estates were ranked against the smaller but influential group of Catholic gentry, the so-called Spanish side, which supported Habsburg rule unequivocally. Although the reformers succeeded in obtaining an Imperial Charter on Freedom of Religion from Rudolf, shortly afterwards the monarch, now worn down by illness and powerless, gave up the political battle against his younger brother Matthias, and

died shortly afterwards in 1612. In 1614 the imposing Matthias Gate (Matyášova brána) was erected at the castle. The gate, designed by Italian architect Vincenzo Scamozzi, heralded the arrival in Prague of a new architectural style — the Baroque.

The confrontation between the House of Habsburg and the predominantly Protestant Czech Estates came to a head on 23 May 1618, with the defenestration of two of the emperor's councillors, the Catholics Jaroslav of Martinic and William of Slavata, who were thrown into the castle moat from the second-floor windows of the Palace's Ludvik Wing. The following year the rebellious Estates offered the Bohe-

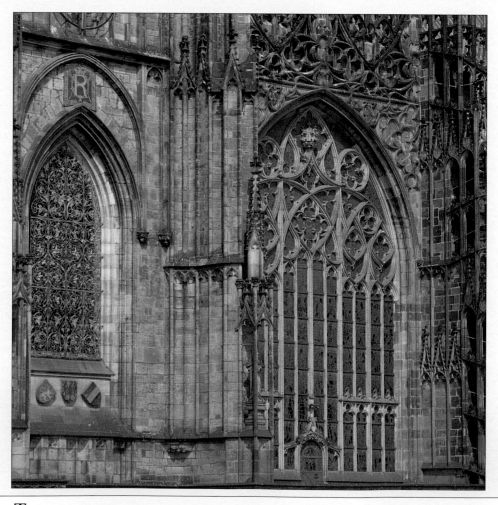

Two more views of St. Vitus' Cathedral. Close to, the graceful work of mediaeval craftsmen and artists and their continuators stands out. Farther off, one can then admire the entire view of the castle, and the jewel in the crown, the Cathedral

44

mian crown to Frederick of the Palatinate, the then leader of the German Protestant Union, who entered Prague on 31 October 1619. The new sovereign, together with his wife Elizabeth, daughter of King James I of England, was crowned King of Bohemia in St. Vitus' Cathedral. However, his reign at Prague Castle lasted only one winter, hence his other title, the "Winter King". With the defeat of the ill-equipped, and above all badly paid troops at White Mountain on 8 November 1620, the uprising by the Czech Estates ended ignominiously. Awaiting anyone who did not manage to escape, carry out a timely conversion, or obtain the intercession of Catholics with the victors, Ferdinand II and the Catholic League, was either a meeting with the executioner on the Old Town Square on 21 June 1621, or, if one was luckier, forced exodus from Mone's homeland, deprived of any means at all. The nation was sub-jugated by administrative and military oppression, and forced re-catholicisation commenced. The victorious Habsburgs then reduced the kingdom of Bohemia to a province devoid of self-government within the Empire.

Shortly before the end of the Thirty Years' War, during which the population in its entirety suffered at the hands of troops from Sweden, Saxony and the Empire itself, the armies under the Swedish General Königsmark succeeded in plundering Rudolf's collections and other treasures located in the castle and the Lesser Quarter. In spite of this, also before the Thirty Years' War came to an end, Ferdinand III began the construction of a new palace according to a design by Giuseppe Mattei. In 1680 the monastic Church of St. George obtained its Baroque gable façade with a relief of the saint, and the chapter provost's residence also gained its Baroque appearance. In the 1720s the two-level Chapel of St. John Nepomuk was added to the Baroque façade of the Church. The Renaissance Lobkowicz Palace (Lobkovický palác) was renovated in Baroque style in the 1670s; and at the end of that century the northern end of the castle and gardens were encircled by a continuous line of Baroque fortifications. Building work on St. Vitus' Cathedral, which had been interrupted, was recom-menced when Emperor Leopold I, perhaps convinced by the prophecy that whosoever completed the con-struction of the Cathedral would oust the Turks from Europe, laid the foundation stone for completion of the Cathedral. In addition to the erection of palaces and religious buildings, the castle witnessed the con-struction of many smaller chapels, and exteriors and interiors were embellished by numerous Baroque sculptures and paintings. At the close of the 17th cen-tury, in the reign of Leopold I, a large manège was built by architect Jean-Baptiste Mathey to the north of Stag Moat.

However, the castle subsequently sustained exten-sive damage as a result of the wars over the Austrian succession and the Seven Years' War, during which it was bombarded by enemy troops. Particularly serious damage was caused during the siege of Prague in 1744, and by fire from Prussian artillery in 1757. Des-pite this, large-scale reconstruction of the castle, fol-lowing the Neoclassical model used in Italy and Vienna, had already been initiated in 1753, in the reign of Empress Maria Theresa, under the direction of the Viennese builder Niccolò Francesco Leonardo Paccassi. This large-scale construction of new castle palaces gave the castle panorama an impressive, al-most classical appearance. Hence the Baroque era at the castle came to a close with monumental building work, and the Neoclassical era had begun.

Yet it was not until the 19th century that the con-tinually delayed intention of completing St. Vitus' Ca-thedral was realised. Under the influence of the pa-triotic Canon Pešina of Čechorod, the Association for the Completion of St. Vitus' Cathedral was founded, and on 1 October 1873 the foundation stone was laid for building work which was to last until 1929. Pac-cassi's construction of castle palaces, and the subse-quent completion of the Cathedral, gave Prague Castle the appearance it retains today.

Following the creation of an independent Czechoslovakia in 1918, Prague Castle was made the seat the President of the Republic. The castle is the most important monument in Prague, the cultural symbol of an historic tradition and the current period of freedom. No visitor to Prague, Czech or foreign, can resist a visit to the castle complex, and, at least in spirit, pays his or her respects to it as a symbol of Czech history and the seat of the President of the Czech Republic.

The Royal Summer Palace (Královský letohrádek) — the most beautiful Renaissance
building north of the Alps. Its design was elaborated by
architect Paolo della Stella

47

The most famous and most admired view of Prague Castle and St. Vitus' Cathedral,
with the Charles Bridge (Karlův most) uniting the Prague towns
on either side of the Vltava

48

HRADČANY

The Martinic Palace (Martinický palác) on Hradčanské náměstí was constructed in 1583 in Renaissance style. The *sgraffito* figures and ornamentation on the façade have been preserved, as have a number of interior ceiling frescoes

Because at the time of the battle fought before Prague Castle in the reign of Henry of Carinthia this was still an open space, the origins of Hradčany and the town must be sought in the days of King John. And yet Hradčany was not initially a royal town, but a humble little town belonging to the burgrave of Prague. For that reason it appears most likely to me that it was founded by a burgrave of Prague with the aim of increasing income from the possessions pertaining to that position. Furthermore, it seems certain that the man was Hynek Berka of Dubá, who occupied that post for the greatest amount of time under King John, and who was, at the same time, administrator of the country.

FROM THE BOOK ON THE HISTORY OF PRAGUE
BY VÁCLAV VLADIVOJ TOMEK

A romantic shot of Hradčanské náměstí (Hradčany Square). The Schwarzenberg Palace
(Schwarzenberský palác), the essence of pure Renaissance construction, was built
by architect Agostino Galli and dates from the mid-16th century

Vladislav II founded the Premonstratensian Strahov Monastery (Strahovský klášter) and its Church of the Assumption (kostel Nanebevzetí Panny Marie) in 1140. It owes its current appearance to later, large-scale Baroque remodelling

52

One of the oldest settlements around Prague probably came into being on the land west of Prague Castle. There the terrain rises slightly from the castle site and widens into an open space demarcated by natural inclines to the north and south. The original settlement on the slope in the castle district may date back as far as the 11th century, although convincing evidence of this is lacking. In any case, some time after 1320, the leading Prague burgrave, Hynek Berka of Dubá, founded the small, partially enclosed town of Hradčany, which was entered through one of three gates. The small town saw the arrival not only of craftsmen, castle servants and clergymen, but also of noblemen, as their duties at the court and St. Vitus' Cathedral required that they be close at hand at all times. Mention is made in the Hradčany town register in 1353 of the Parish Church of St. Benedict, which stood on the southwest corner of what is now Hradčanské náměstí (Hradčany Square).

Following the erection of Charles' fortifications encompassing the area on Prague's left bank, a suburb known as Pohořelec, because of its of having been swept by fire, was founded in 1375 by the deputy burgrave, Aleš of Malkovice, west of the original Strahov Gate in Hradčany, between the fortifications of the Strahov Monastery and Charles' new wall. The new walls themselves also covered the area northwest of Hradčany where, in Rudolf II's reign, a new area of the castle district — the picturesque Nový Svět (New World) — developed.

Disaster struck for Hradčany when the Hussite Revolution began, since during the fighting for control of Prague Castle the little town was burnt down and demolished, for the most part by the Hussites, and to a lesser extent by the royal garrison. It took the Hradčany area a long time to recover from the damage it sustained; it was the construction work undertaken on the Castle under the House of Jagellon which first brought the little town back to life. During that period the first, modest town hall was built on the upper part of Hradčanské náměstí. Pohořelec, meanwhile, remained desolate.

The large fire which engulfed the Lesser Quarter and spread to the castle and Hradčany in 1541 slowed the growth of the small town, reducing most of the newly erected or inhabited houses to ashes. After the Estates' revolt was put down, Hradčany too witnessed the execution of those accused of participating in the resistance movement on Hradčanské náměstí. Only in the mid-16th century did Hradčany begin to flourish once more;

The most eye-catching part of the façade of the Archbishop's Palace is the large coat of arms of a former Archbishop of Prague, Antonín Příchovský, with whose funds the reconstruction of the palace, as it still looks today, was carried out

53

the culmination of this renaissance came in 1598, when the district was elevated to royal town status. Naturally, the burghers erected a new, Renaissance town hall further to the right, where Loretánská ulice (Loretto Street) meets Hradčanské náměstí. That period saw the construction in Hradčany of magnificent renaissance palaces for the nobility, for example Lobkowicz (later Schwarzenberg) Palace, Gryspek Palace, purchased later for the Prague archbishopric restored by Ferdinand I, or the house of Christopher Popel of Lobkowicz (later Šternberk Palace).

During the Thirty Years' War and other hostilities, the town of Hradčany was never spared the destructive rampages of a whole series of armies. In spite of this, the Hradčany of today is the telling proof of the beauty of Prague's Renaissance, Baroque and more recent architectural styles. The most attractive area of the castle district is, of course, Hradčanské náměstí, a vast space enclosed by palaces and ancient structures. The north side of the square is dominated by the Archbishop's Palace; construction begun in 1562 on the foundations of the original Renaissance Gryspek Palace, when the Prague archbishopric once again had an occupant in Antonín Brus of Mohelnice. The palace underwent further significant structural modifications under Archbishop Jan Bedřich of Waldstein: it was given an early Baroque appearance by the architect Jean-Baptiste Mathey. The Baroque main entrance to the palace and bower have been preserved to this day; nonetheless, the building looks now as it would have done after the reconstruction effected by the architect Johann Josef Wirch in 1764—1765, financed by Archbishop Antonín Příchovský. The magnificent huge palace façade and its light Rococo décor are reflected substantially in the vista of Prague Castle and Hradčany.

Through the passage on the left wing of the Archbishop's Palace one reaches the Šternberk Palace, a significant baroque structure built for Wenceslas Adalbert of Šternberk by architects Giovanni Battista Alliprandi and Giovanni Santini, which is the currently home to the National Gallery of European Art. The collections featuring the Italian school of painters, the old Dutch masters and Renaissance paintings from outside Italy are notable for their scope and comprehensiveness, whilst the collection of German masters is particularly impressive. A separate section houses a collection of 19th- and 20th-century French painters.

Further along the north side of the square stands a row of Baroque houses of canons in the St. Vitus chapter, which ends with the Martinic Palace, situated on the corner of the square where it meets Kanovnická ulice (Canon Street). The Martinic family purchased the unfinished palace in 1583, and thanks to their care it became into a true gem of the Renaissance. In the mid-1600s its then owner, Helena Barbara Kostomlatská of Vřesovice, widow of Jaroslav of Martinic, had the building adapted. Proceeding down the street one reaches the Baroque Church of St. John Nepomuk, a stunning structure by Kilian Ignaz Dienzenhofer dating from 1720—1729, and adjacent to it the Ursuline convent. The magnificent frescoes depicting scenes from the life of St. John Nepomuk which grace the church's interior are the work of Václav Reiner, dating back to 1727—1728.

The entire west side of Hradčanské náměstí is taken up by the frontal of the Palace of the Dukes of Tuscany; its Italian Baroque façade dominates the whole area. Giovanni Antonio Canevalle built the palace between 1689 and 1691 for its prospective owner, Count Michal Oswald Thun. Its architect is believed to have been the Burgundian Jean-Baptiste Mathey.

The south side is occupied by the two Schwarzenberg Palaces, of which the larger, with its pretty, ornamented gables, *sgraffito* decoration and imitation brickwork, dates from the second half of the 16th century and is the work of the builder Agostino Galli. It is one of the best examples of the adoption of Italian Renaissance architecture in Bohemia. The other palace, opposite the castle at the end of the square, is Neoclassical, dating from the early 1800s, and was paid for by Archbishop Vilém Florentin Salm-Salm. Two thoroughfares converge beyond the former Carmelite convent grounds in the southwest corner of the square. The first, for pedestrians, the broad, so-called Town Hall Steps, lead one through pretty twists and turns and passages to the Lesser Quarter; the second, Loretánská, is the main artery in Hradčany. At their point of intersection stands a late Renaissance building, once Hradčany Town Hall. The street, lined for the most part with Renaissance and Baroque palaces and buildings, leads into Loretánské náměstí (Loretto Square), the name of which derives from the shrine. The central feature of this vast area is the Santa Casa (Holy House, in Czech, Svatý domek), built as a reproduction of a project by the architect Bramante for the original house in Loretto, Italy. Prague's Santa Casa was erected in 1626—1627 by Giovanni Battista Orsi; the

This part of Hradčany is called Nový Svět (New World), and is one of
the most romantic and picturesque
areas of Prague

55

funds were provided by Benigna, Countess of Lobkowicz. Cloisters, built initially on one level, and subsequently on two levels with seven chapels, encircle the house. Kristof Dientzenhofer participated in the extension work on the main chapel along the axis of the building in the 1720s; the result of this was the Church of the Nativity, and it was Dientzenhofer's son, Kilian Ignaz, who worked on the extension and adaptation of the church. Every hour the famous bells of the Loretto tower chime "We Greet Thee, Mary, a Thousand Times", a melody inextricably linked to the Hradčany atmosphere. The Loretto also houses a wide collection of ceremonial garments and vessels dating back to the Renaissance and Baroque periods. One symbol of the place, as well as of the Loretto Treasury, is the famous diamond monstrance, the Prague Sun. It was designed by Viennese architect Johann Bernhard Fischer von Erlach, and is set with six and a half thousand diamonds. The oldest gold collection piece is a late Gothic chalice bearing enamel figures of early-16th century Czech patrons.

In contrast to the Baroque splendour of the Loretto is the great simplicity of the nearby Capuchin Monastery, founded in 1600 on land owned by Margaret of Lobkowicz. Cannon balls are implanted in the wall of the small church of Our Lady of Angels, a reminder of the bombardment of Prague by the Prussian army led by Frederick the Great during the wars with Maria Theresa over succession to the Austrian throne. The little church's interior is perfectly coordinated, and at Christmas time many visitors come to see its famous "Nativity scene".

The entire north side of Loretánské náměstí is occupied by the awesome, solidly-sculpted façade of the Černín Palace, designed and erected for Count Humprecht Černín by Francesco Caratti between 1669 and 1677 with the assistance of Giovanni Decapauli and Abraham Leuther. The Count's descendants continued the adaptations to, and decoration of the Palace into the 18th century; in 1742 and 1757 the palace suffered serious damage, firstly at the hands of the French army, and then from Prussian bombardment. In 1851 it was sold to the public treasury and converted into a barracks. The devastated palace was then taken over by the Czechoslovak state in 1918, and in 1934 the carefully restored building was given to the foreign ministry.

To the north of the palace lies Nový Svět, a charming little suburb of Hradčany containing pretty little houses of Baroque appearance and smaller palaces, whilst to the west the triangular Pohořelec Square is situated. On the upper right-hand corner of Pohořelec stands the Kučera Palace, originally called The Golden Boat (U Zlaté lodi) or the Demartins'. The extraordinary façade was most probably the creation of Johann Josef Wirch. In the lower part of Pohořelec nad Úvozem stands St. Elizabeth's Hospital, an interesting building from the latter half of the 17th century constructed for the abbot of Strahov Monastery, Vincenc Frank. Steps with the sculptural group entitled Calvary lead up to a raised portal, the dominant feature of the façade. Of particular interest is the south side of the square, whose buildings adjoin those of the former Strahov brewery and continue as far as the Baroque gateway to the Strahov Monastery grounds, adorned with a statue of St. Norbert. Close by stands the beautiful Gothic-Renaissance Church of St. Roch, erected on a design by Giovanni Maria Fillippi in the reign of Rudolf.

King Vladislav founded the monastery in 1140 at the initiative of Jindřich Zdík, Bishop of Olomouc, and placed in it the new Premonstratensian Order. The royal establishment of the monastery is demonstrated both by the strategic importance of the site — the name Strahov derives from the word "guard", and from the hill it was possible to control access to the castle and town from the west — and by the extraordinary size and architectural richness of the walled-in grounds. Strahov Monastery ranked amongst the richest in the country, was celebrated as a seat of educational brilliance, and was the centre of the Order's jurisdiction. Its nucleus is the abbot's Church of the Assumption, originally a Romanesque basilica dating back to the 12th century, though it obtained its current appearance as a result of Gothic, Baroque and Renaissance reconstruction.

The most valuable treasure housed by the monastery is its library. Contained within it is an extraordinary range of manuscripts (the oldest parchment dates from the 9th century), incunabula, more recent theological works and others of the natural sciences and the humanities. The greater part of the library's contents is located in historic interiors which still boast their original decoration and furniture. After decades of forced isolation, the Premonstratensians are once again returning to the monastery.

Strahov Monastery affords a breathtaking view of the city, dominated to the left by Prague Castle, and to the right by the green slopes of Petřín Hill.

A preserved fragment of Renaissance decoration on the façade of Hradčany Town Hall
(Hradčanská radnice) in the lower part of Loretánská
ulice (Loretto Street)

Where Loretánská ulice (Loretto Street) leads into Hradčanské náměstí, Hradčany Town Hall (Hradčanská radnice) was erected. The original Renaissance structure was adapted in Baroque style in the first half of the 18th century

This is a fabulous view of Prague's Loretto with the famous Santa Casa
(Holy House, in Czech, Svatý domek) dating from 1626, the bell
tower, and the Loretto Treasury (Loretánský poklad)

The Strahov Monastery (Strahovský klášter) and its Church of the Assumption
(kostel Nanebevzetí Panny Marie) rank amongst the oldest
and most valuable of Prague's religious monuments

Through the gateway leading into the grounds of Strahov Monastery, dominated by a statue
to St. Norbert, stands the unassuming little Church of St. Roch
(kostel sv. Rocha), which dates from 1603—1612

The Old Town Square (Staroměstské náměstí) has long been the natural centre of the town. The towers on the Church of Our Lady Before Týn (kostel Panny Marie před Týnem) rise up high above the houses of city-dwellers and the palaces of the nobility

PRAGUE OLD TOWN

The Old Town Hall. A section of the heraldic decoration on the southeastern corner of the Gothic Town Hall chapel from the latter half of the 14th century

In the first year of his reign, and for years afterwards, King Wenceslas bestowed great favours upon the secular and regular clergy alike, and with still greater fondness he venerated the churches of God and their servants. However, subsequently, when his father had already passed away, he had the town of Prague surrounded by a wall, and saw to it that other market villages — which in our common language are called towns — were fortified with wood or stone.

Whilst he was sovereign, good peace reigned for many years .

FROM THE CONTINUATION OF THE CHRONICLE OF COSMAS

63

The tall tower of the Old Town Hall (Staroměstská radnice), dating from the period
when Gothic style was at its height, is the prominent feature
of this part of the Old Town Square

The Art Nouveau monument to Jan Hus (John Huss), unveiled at the beginning of the 20th century, and the Baroque Church of St. Nicholas, dating from the 1730s, are two of the most important monuments on the Old Town Square

The origins of an unbroken settlement on the right bank of the Vltava river can be traced back to the close of the 10th century. The axes of the settlement represented the routes leading to fords over the Vltava, and probably to the first predecessor of the Charles Bridge, namely a wooden structure, over which the body of the murdered Prince Wenceslas was supposedly carried to Prague Castle. The records of the chronicler Cosmas from 1091, which allude to mercantile settlements in the area below the castle, indicate that the first of them may well have been situated in the foreground immediately adjacent to the castle, with the second on the route connecting Vyšehrad and the ford over the river, somewhere between the present-day Mánes Bridge and the Charles Bridge. From there, the route then continued on to Prague Castle. This would also account for the growing importance of the area on the right bank after the temporary transfer of the prince's residence to Vyšehrad in the reign of Vratislav II. That place was inhabited at the time by a community of German traders, and probably by others too, as is suggested by Cosmas' account of the famous arrival in Prague of Břetislav II in 1092, in which he tells of "the dancing crowds at various crossroads and in the churches beneath the castle".

At the end of the 11th century the marketplace alluded to by the chronicler was most likely located somewhere in the area now called the Old Town Square (Staroměstské náměstí). Still later than 1100 it was the place where in addition to Saturday markets, public gatherings took place and armies were assembled when the need arose. For instance, in 1105 the army of Prince Svatopluk set up camp "at the large marketplace between Prague [Castle] and Vyšehrad".

Indeed, after 1100 the area situated below the castle entered a new stage of development, culminating in the commencement of the construction of the town walls in 1230. The population of Romanesque Prague was concentrated above all around the marketplace and between the present-day Perštýn crossroads and the wooden bridge, replaced by the stone Judith Bridge in about 1170.

This concentrated settlement began to take shape in around the mid-1100s, and by the early 13th century the old town settlement, known as podhradí Pražské (Beneath Prague Castle) or Mezihradí (Between the Castles), contained the most marked settlement formation in the entire Prague area. A flurry of economic activity and the increased wealth of many inhabitants stimulated building activity, and subsequently influenced population growth, which relied upon large-scale immigration and was an accompanying sign of prosperity. The existence of perma-

The late Gothic portal on the Old Town Hall with its sculpted flowers and crabs was built during the reign of the House of Jagellon

The Astronomical Clock (orloj). The famous painted calendar
with its allegories of the months
is by Josef Mánes

QVI DEDIT
HAEC VETERI TVRRITA
INSIGNIA PRAGAE
OMINA VENTVRAE SORTIS·
AMICA DEDIT MOLE SVA VT
CELSAE TRANSCENDVNT
MOENIA TVRRES
SIC FAMAM SVPERAS
INCLITA PRAGA TVAM
MDCXIV Martinus Cuthen

PRAGA·CAPVT·REGNI

OMNIA TVRRIGERAE
CONCEDVNT OPPIDA PRAGAE
NATVRA HIC POSVIT
QVIDQVID IN ORBE FVIT
HIC GENVS ACRE VIRVM
BONVS AER VNDA SALVBRIS
AD VITEM ET FRVGES
INGENIOSVS AGER
HIC CAESAR PROCERESQVE
THEMISQVE NOVVMQVE SCROBES
HIC ALIIS SPRETIS ORBIS
IN VRBE SVA EST
Julius Scaliger

The latin inscription *Praga caput regni* ("Prague, head of the kingdom")
on the Old Town Hall bears testimony to the town's importance,
its wealth and its political aspirations

nent resting places for foreign traders, facilitated by privileges bestowed by the prince, strengthened the importance of the marketplace. Foreign traders found shelter at the prince's large Týn Court, the first mention of which is made during the reign of Prince Bořivoj II. Here import and transit duty, the "Ungelt" was collected, hence the courtyard became known by that same title. The court also provided traders with accommodation and enabled them to rest after a weary journey, thereby also earning it the Latin name curia laeta, (jolly courtyard), or hospitum.

The architectural richness of a large portion of the area lying below the castle on the right bank of the river, the concentration around the main marketplace, the formation of a street network, and other elements besides, determined the urban nature of the settlement from the mid-12th century onwards. Despite the rapid upsurge in building activity in Romanesque Prague, a sizeable population and expanding trade and craftsmanship, no universally-binding legal norms which might influence the collective life of the settlement as a whole had as yet been applied. Nevertheless, it was precisely this important sign that differentiated mediaeval towns from less developed communities.

The erection of walls commenced by King Wenceslas I after 1230 was the key event in the process of transforming the settlement beneath the castle into the town of Prague, or as it was initially called with reference to the castle, civitas Pragensis. Yet the significance of the walls was more than military; they also marked the strengthening of the internal and external unity of the town, and thus created the important legal and social preconditions for the collective development of town life.

The walls surrounding the new town stretched for 1700 metres and enclosed an area of some 140 hectares. The double wall was reinforced by a number of towers, a good few of them as many as thirty metres tall, and entry into the town was guarded by gates.

At around the same time, during completion of the settlement, a number of predominantly German settlers founded St. Gall's Town, an enclave which for some time retained its administrative independence. The walls were completed by 1241, and with that the external changes to the settlement below the castle also came to an end. Irrespective of the walls' military function, the fortified town became an altogether different settlement from the previous scattered, partial communities. Craftsmanship and trade within the town expanded rapidly, monasteries were constructed, and other markets, besides the main one, sprang up.

The arrival of the Gothic style in Prague and Bohemia as a whole is symbolised by an act of foundation executed by King Wenceslas I. In 1233 he provided an extensive

The sign on Prague's first Cubist house, designed by Josef Gočár, is a statuette of a Black Madonna in a golden cage

The Renaissance building, The Two Golden Bears on Kožná Lane, the childhood home of the well-known journalist and writer, Egon Ervín Kisch

Jan Hus. This grand Art Nouveau monument on the Old Town Square was the creation
of Ladislav Šaloun. The Neo-Baroque Art Nouveau buildings in the background
date from the late 19th and 20th centuries

70

area for the construction of a convent for the Poor Clares. The Order had been introduced into the country by the king's sister, St. Agnes of Bohemia (sv. Anežka Česká), the first abbess of the convent. Although the convent was originally intended for the Poor Clares alone, a section of it was later set aside also for their brother community, the Franciscans. Agnes' activity was reflected both in the erection of the convent, which lasted half a century, and in the nation's spiritual, cultural and political life. The educated princess rejected offers of advantageous dynastic marriages, preferring to serve Christ, the poor and the sick. Her vision, contacts and diplomatic abilities made her a leading figure of the 13th century.

Prague's rapid expansion occurred in the reign of Přemysl Otakar II. According to a contemporary historian, Prague, "particularly in his reign, succeeded in becoming very rich and affluent, thanks in part to the lively activity at a busy court and the vastness of Otakar's empire . . . also giving foreigners from far and wide a reason for visiting the capital". Trade and weekly markets were controlled by domestic traders, and under pressure exerted by craftsmen — a sizeable social stratum in themselves by the close of the 13th century — an urban trade system began to take shape, the mainstay of which were the guilds.

An extraordinary amount of building work was undertaken in the town, above all from the latter half of the

13th century onwards. At this time the Monastery and Church of St. James (klášter a kostel sv. Jakuba) were constructed, rebuilding began on the Church of Our Lady Before Týn (kostel Panny Marie před Týnem), and the erection of St. Agnes' Convent (klášter sv. Anežky) got under way. The Dominican Order founded the Church of St. Clement's (kostel sv. Klimenta) near the Judith Bridge, and adjacent to it the Knights of the Cross with the Red Star established their own monastery.

The upsurge in trade and production under Přemysl Otakar II created favourable conditions for the increase in the property holdings and financial means of a section of the population. The rapid material and social rise of the town patricians, profiting also from their share in silver mining and transactions in precious metals, led to an expansion in land development by the population. Here, too, the Gothic style gradually imposed its forms, measures and dimensions, albeit with greater difficulty than in the construction of religious buildings.

The process leading to the internal unification of the town reached full maturity in around 1287. By then the town was headed by a royal magistrate, who as a rule oversaw the town judiciary and administration with twelve councillors appointed by the king. It is interesting to note that in the same year King Wenceslas II imposed a ban upon the carrying of weapons in the town, although it

The tombstone of Tycho Brahe, who spent the last years of his life in exile at the court of Emperor Rudolf II. He was buried in the Church of Our Lady Before Týn in 1601

71

A view of Old Town towers and housetops from the Old Town Bridge Tower (Staroměstská mostecká věž). In the immediate foreground are the dome of the Church of St. Francis (kostel sv. Františka) and the façade of the Church of the Holy Saviour (kostel sv. Salvátora) on Křížovnické náměstí (Knights of the Cross Square)

The façade of the Church of St. James (kostel sv. Jakuba) is dominated by this late-seventeenth century relief of St. James by Ottavio Mosto

One of the new shops which have sprung up in lanes around the Old Town
recently, and which have brought this historic area
of Prague back to life

73

The façade of the Neo-Renaissance Rott House (dům U Rotta) on Malé náměstí (Little
Square) with its beautiful fountain is decorated with frescoes taken
from designs by Mikoláš Aleš

was not observed for long. Nuremberg law was considered the legal basis for unification, yet this rôle was, in fact, played by the so-called "Swabian mirror", which underwent local modifications and made concessions in line with Magdeburg law. Even after unification, the town as a whole did not become a unified entity, since small areas remained under the jurisdiction of the Church authorities.

In spite of their increased wealth, the inhabitants failed to weaken the rôle of the royal magistrate and strengthen the influence of the councillors. Nor did Wenceslas II yield to the burghers when asked in 1296 to grant permission for the establishment of a town hall, although on the whole he did favour the towns and generally supported their development. The king's unwillingness stemmed from his mistrust of the freedom of towns. As their wealth steadily increased at the beginning of the 14th century, the patricians began to harbour constantly greater political ambitions, which now extended beyond the town boundaries. When Wenceslas III died in 1306, and the last of the male heirs of the Přemysl dynasty with him, the Prague nobles finally split into two rival groups, the first of which, led by the Velflovitz family, supported Henry of Carinthia as candidate for the Bohemian throne, whilst the Olbramovic family and others championed the Habsburg claim. The fierce struggle for power and influence with regard to the future ruler of Bohemia resulted in the town's being deprived of the peace required for economic life, and its becoming instead the scene of many clashes and battles. The struggle for Prague in the early 1300s also demonstrated, however, that the fortification system was so successful that it was possible to gain control of the town only with the help of allies within its walls.

The victory of John of Luxemburg in the struggle for the Bohemian crown brought the town the peace it had long desired. Nonetheless, it became immediately apparent that the king would constantly be seeking finances in the form of gifts or non-repayable loans. The citizens of Prague had already presented the royal couple with expensive jewellery amounting to 120 talents of silver at their coronation, but this was merely the beginning. Having said that, the magnanimous Luxemburg repaid the inhabitants of Prague with new privileges, eventually granting them permission to establish their own town hall on 18 September 1338 whilst away in Amiens. This was the culmination of the inhabitants' previous attempts to win self-government, and when in 1341 the king furthermore gave them his consent to draw up their own legal code and gave the Prague town hall judicial sovereignty over the other towns, he was acknowledging the exceptional status of the town within the realm. The burghers then immediately bought a corner house at the marketplace, and established their town hall there.

In 1346 John of Luxemburg's son, Charles IV, was elected King of Rome, and in that same year ascended the Bohemian throne after his father was killed at the Battle of Crécy. With that Prague suddenly became a genuine residential town, as the new monarch's subsequent building activities confirmed.

Charles' many creative deeds did not leave the Old Town untouched. First of all, in 1348 he founded a university there, in order that, as one may read in the university's foundation charter, "the inhabitants of the kingdom of Bohemia should not be forced to beg for alms in foreign lands, but should find in the realm a table set for their needs". During the life of its founder, the university, the first of its kind north of the Alps, began to attract scholars from lands under the Bohemian crown, as well as from neighbouring and more distant parts of Christendom, and became a focus for spiritual fervour.

In the early 15th century, Prague's Charles University (Karlova univerzita) emerged as a centre of intellectual opposition which responded to the crises in society, and simultaneously mobilised and united malcontents from various social strata in Prague and the kingdom as a whole. The attitudes of Czech masters (professors) were based to a great extent on the views expressed by English reformer John Wycliffe, many of whose writings were brought to Bohemia by Jerome of Prague.

The official administration of Charles University has been, and is to this day, directed from the Carolinum (Karolinum), the nucleus of which was the oldest building, the Gothic Rothlev House, belonging to the master of the mint and dating from the latter half of the 14th century. The large assembly hall with the oriel chapel, and the Gothic porticos at ground level, have been preserved to this day. A statue of Jan Hus by the sculptor Karel Lidický stands in the quadrangle.

In 1357 Charles IV began construction of a new stone bridge spanning the Vltava. It was designed to replace the Judith Bridge, destroyed by floods, and connect the Prague towns on the river's right bank with the Lesser Quarter, as it was known after 1348, the year in which the

Visitors to Prague also gather
on the illuminated Old Town Square
in the evening and enjoy an attractive ride
in a horse-and-carriage

king founded the New Town outside the walls of the larger town, the Old Town, on the strip of land extending along the river bank from Vyšehrad to Poříčí (river basin) in the New Town. The construction of the bridge and the imposing Old Town Bridge Tower demonstrated the mastery of Peter Parler and his workshop. Charles IV entrusted care of the bridge and its defence to the Old Town burghers, and also placed under Old Town administrative control the sizeable bridgehead encompassing Kampa Island, or as it was then known, Ostrov (The Isle).

Even after the New Town had been established, the more prominent members of the nobility and the wealthier burgher families remained in the Old Town, a bastion of trade. Thus, in order to emphasise its greater importance, Charles IV increased the number of Old Town councillors from twelve to eighteen. Building activity there was intense; the town hall tower with its chapel containing an oriel window was erected, and the affluence of the burghers was reflected in the predominance of new houses with a large parlour. Moreover, the royal court was built in the Old Town. Practically every church in the Old Town was reconstructed; the Gothicising process was evident in the extensive reconstruction project undertaken on the Church of Our Lady Before Týn, and in the revamping of the Church and Franciscan Monastery of St. James, the Church of St. Gall (kostel sv. Havla), the Church of St. Giles (kostel sv. Jiljí), and other churches situated in the Old Town. Little by little Charles' notion of a residential royal seat was becoming reality. The town's population was on the increase and Prague, dominated by the Old Town, profited from the economic prosperity that characterised Charles' reign.

However, population density brought with it the danger of a large section of the wage-earners, who came to Prague in search of work when the town first began to prosper fully, finding themselves unable to earn a sufficiently decent livelihood. Disagreements also emerged between patricians and craftsmen, who wished to exploit their increased economic wealth in order to gain greater influence over the administration of the town. The differences were further exacerbated under Charles' son, Wenceslas IV, above all after 1400, when Prague ceased to be the seat of the King of the Romans, and the period during which it had flourished under the great emperor became a thing of the past. A number of building projects begun in Charles'

reign remained unfinished, craftsmen and merchants saw their trade diminish, and fewer job opportunities became available to less affluent citizens. Prague's retreat from the political limelight demonstrated its reliance on local consumption, the decline in which hit every stratum of the population. These unpleasant circumstances aggravated existing internal disputes amongst its citizens.

The aforesaid notwithstanding, the Old Town's economy stood on firm foundations, and as a consequence it suffered fewer negative effects of the economic stagnation than the New Town, where a higher proportion of craftsmen and poorer wage-earners were situated. It was no coincidence, therefore, that the Hussite Revolution broke out precisely in the New Town, for here thought as to how to put matters right was more liable to be translated into action. Furthermore, in the course of the revolution the demands laid down by the New Town were consistently more radical than those of the Old Town.

In the aftermath of the Battle of Lipany in 1434, with the Old Town in the hands of the victors and the New Town on the losing side, the administrators of the Old Town played a significant part in the succession of Sigismund of Luxemburg to the throne of Bohemia. He duly repaid them by restoring former privileges and granting new ones. During the interregnum which ensued from the death of Albert of Habsburg, Sigismund's son-in-law and successor to the Bohemian throne, the rôle of the Old Town as centre of the realm increased immeasurably. The rise in the Old Town burghers' political power was confirmed by the fact that in 1458 the Old Town Hall was the place in which a new ruler for Bohemia, George of Poděbrady, was elected from amongst the ranks of the Utraquist nobles.

In the reign of the House of Jagellon, the Old Town maintained its privileged position at the head of the town Estates in the realm, though to this end it had to put up a fierce fight against the nobility within the Estates-General. Over the same period, another unprecedented upsurge in building activities in the town was seen. The important political rôle played by the burghers in the post-Hussite Estates-General, and their wealth, corresponded also to the high cultural level of their environment. The late Gothic style, expressed in the works of master architects Benedict Ried and Matěj Rejsek, left its indelible marks on the town. The adaptations to, and reconstruction and enlargement of the Old Town Hall, the remodelling of the Astronomical Clock by Master Hanuš in about 1490, and the erection of a so-called New Tower at

The pretty little Church of the Holy Saviour (kostel sv. Salvátora), dating from the latter half of the 13th century, forms part of St. Agnes' Convent (klášter sv. Anežky)

the Old Town royal court — the Powder Tower (Prašná brána) as we know it today, commenced in 1475 under the supervision of Prague builder Wenceslas and completed by Matěj Rejsek — stand out above all in this respect. Architectural activity was resumed on the monastery of the Knights of the Cross with the Red Star near the Charles Bridge, and the Bethlehem Chapel (Betlémská kaple), a reminder of Jan Hus, was also adapted in late Gothic style. Construction work proceeded on the burghers' houses, too, with architectural adaptations focused in the main on the central area of the Old Town, and above all on residences belonging to the Old Town nobility.

After the Habsburgs' succession to the Bohemian throne, the new ruler, Ferdinand I, began systematically to curb the status enjoyed by the town, and in 1534 he also put an end to the temporary joint administration of the Old and New Towns by councillors. Ferdinand's policy towards the town provoked disaffection, and opposition to the monarch amongst the citizens of Prague grew steadily. Differences came to a head in 1547, when the Old Town, other royal towns and the majority of Bohemian nobles refused military support to Ferdinand, who was engaged in helping his brother, Emperor Charles V, in his war against the so-called pro-reform Schmalkalden League. However, the resistance movement was badly led and ended in a disaster for the people of Prague without precedent in the town's history. The town's inhabitants were the first victims of Ferdinand's harsh justice.

Sixt of Ottersdorf, the Chancellor of the Old Town who later chronicled these events, was threatened with execution, a great many burghers were imprisoned or banished from the country, and still more had their property confiscated. Municipal administrations in the royal towns were made subordinate to the royal magistrates, and in the Old and New Towns to the royal provosts also. With the defeat of the resistance movement Prague's status, built up over many years, collapsed overnight. The town's political heyday and its important role amongst the Estates had come to an end.

In the late 1500s and early 1600s Prague still retained its Gothic character, but Renaissance architecture was gradually creeping into the town. Well-to-do citizens possessed the resources with which to match the nobility in terms of the architectural richness of their homes and their lifestyle. Proof of this is shown by the stunning, *sgraffito*-decorated House At the Minute (U Minuty) beside the town hall buildings, The Two Golden Bears (U Dvou zlatých medvědů) with its superb portal, The French Crown (U Francouzské koruny) in Karlova ulice (Charles Street), where astronomer Johannes Kepler once lived, the Týn School (Týnská škola) on the Old Town Square, or the Granovský House (dům Granovských) behind the Týn Church. The Renaissance style was introduced into religious building work by the Jesuits during construction of the Church of the Holy Saviour (kostel sv. Salvátora) and the Italian Chapel (Vlašská kaple), and the style was also evident in the interiors of other sacred buildings, such as the Church of Our Lady before Týn.

When forces from Passau invaded in 1611, the inhabitants of the Old Town distinguished themselves in their defence of the town against the army led by Colonel Ramée. With its help, Emperor Rudolf II, at the end of his reign, had hoped to reverse his unfavourable position vis-à-vis the Bohemian Estates and his brother Matthias. In the years that ensued, the town played centre stage to many dramatic incidents. The Old Town citizens joined in the anti-Habsburg uprising in 1618, but although Prague found itself in the midst of all events, its inhabitants themselves remained on the fringe. Furthermore, in spite of their involvement in the revolt, they failed to obtain satisfaction for certain demands they had made on the leaders of the nobles' Estates. The short reign of Frederick of the Palatinate ended in defeat at the Battle of White Mountain, and it was only natural that it should be the burghers who again paid a higher price than the aristocracy for their part in the uprising, despite the fact that their influence over the course of events had been slight. Fifteen of the towns' burghers were executed on 21 June 1621; many others were forced to flee the country; and still more either saw their property taken from them or incurred fines. When non-Catholics were expelled from Prague by decree in 1628, only Catholics and converts who had changed their religious beliefs in order to preserve their livelihood remained, so that when some emigrés returned for a short time during an invasion from Saxony, they were not made welcome. The change in the situation in Prague, and its devotion to the Habsburg monarchy, came to the fore when the Swedes laid seige to the town. The less-than-sturdy walls were defended by the inhabitants of the Old and New Towns, together with a small garrison of the Emperor's army, with practically no artillery. Even the Viennese court acknowledged the citizens' stubborn resistance to the Swedes; however, the political importance of the Prague towns was barely enhanced.

The Estates Theatre (Stavovské divadlo), which dates from the late 18th century, is a splendid
example of Neoclassical architecture. The first performance of
W. A. Mozart's opera Don Giovanni was given here in 1787

Building activity in the town resumed shortly after the end of the Thirty Years' War. From the mid-1600s onwards, palaces for the aristocracy, monasteries and churches sprang up in the new Baroque style. Projects meriting particular attention in this regard are the reconstruction of the Churches of St. James in the Old Town, St. Gall, and SS Simon and Jude, together with the founding of a monastery and hospital, and the construction of a large Jesuit College in the Old Town and other sacred buildings, in which the Baroque style prevailed until the mid-18th century. As a result of their great secular and sacred construction works, the names of the outstanding architects of the Prague Baroque era, such as Kilian Ignaz Dientzenhofer, František Maximilián Kaňka, Jean-Baptiste Mathey, Carlo Lurago, Giovanni Santini-Aichl, Johann Bernard Fischer von Erlach, Giovanni Alliprandi, Jan Josef Hrdlička and others, were written into the history books. Equal in brilliance was Baroque sculpture and painting as embodied by the work of Matthias Braun, Jan Jiří Bendl, Matthias Jäckel, Václav Reiner and Ignaz Platzer, which added the finishing touches to the exteriors and interiors of these structures. Besides the Clam-Gallas Palace on Husova ulice (Huss Street) as it is called today, the magnificent Baroque Church of St. Nicholas on the Old Town Square, or the Jesuit College, these illustrious master builders also worked on the construction of new houses for the burghers. However, here for the most part the new style was applied only to façades, with existing structural layouts remaining unaltered. That period's taste for relief was reflected in the embellishment of numerous portals and the addition of house signs, as seen in Karlova, Celetná (Baker Street) and Rytířská (Knight Street). Between 1683 and 1714 thirty statues were erected on the stone Charles Bridge, the work of leading master sculptors, and in particular Matthias Bernard Braun and Ferdinand Maximilian Brokof.

Construction work undertaken in the Old Town in the second half of the 18th century was also influenced by the Rococo style, which left exquisite façades on many houses of the middle class and palaces belonging to the nobility, the late Baroque Goltz-Kinsky Palace on the Old Town Square serving as one example. However, Rococo soon made way for Neoclassical, characterised by its austere forms and décor, as illustrated by the Estates Theatre in the Old Town. Previously called the Nostitz Theatre in recognition of its benefactor, Count Anton von Nostitz-Rieneck, the plans for the building were drawn up by Antonín Haffenecker. The first performance of Wolfgang Amadeus Mozart's celebrated opera, Don Giovanni, was given here in 1787. In the late 1800s the styles most often employed imitated above all Gothic and Renaissance and, later, Baroque architecture. Yet the most marked influence to exert itself on Prague was the Neo-Renaissance; one of the most splendid buildings erected in that style is the Rudolfinum, constructed on a design by Josef Zítek and Josef Schulz. This remarkable piece of architecture is beautifully located on Dvořákovo nábřeží (Dvořák Embankment), and its façade looks out onto náměstí Jana Palacha (Jan Palach Square). Facing one side of the Rudolfinum, on ulice 17. listopadu (17 November Street) stands the huge edifice which now houses the Museum of Decorative Arts, built between 1897 and 1901 by architect Josef Schulz in French Neo-Renaissance style. Other interesting Neo-Renaissance structures include the former Palace of the Counts Lažanský, built in 1861—1863, and the neighbouring building, the former Czech Savings Bank, erected in 1856—1861. Both were the creation of architect Ignaz Ullmann, and are situated on the Old Town side of Národní třída (National Avenue), opposite the National Theatre (ND).

The small area between the Old and New Towns, through which Národní třída, the street named Na Příkopě (On the Moat) and Revoluční třída run today, was thoroughly rebuilt, and the part of the town adjacent to the bend in the river was altered as a result of redevelopment. The architectural styles prevalent in the latter half of the 19th century, and early-20th century Art Nouveau, influenced the construction of entire building complexes in the Old Town erected in accordance with redevelopment plans. A shining example is Pařížská ulice (Paris Street), which leads directly into the unique Art Nouveau Czech Bridge (Čechův most). There exist a whole series of interesting Art Nouveau buildings in Prague, above all the important Municipal House (Obecní dům), erected between 1905 and 1912 on the site where Charles' court once stood, next to the Powder Tower and the Gothic-Art Nouveau Hotel Paříž, dating from 1907.

Prague Old Town remains to this day a permanent reminder of the rich history of Prague and of Bohemia as a whole. Its current appearance is the result of complex urban development beginning in the Romanesque period and extending into the recent past. Both the Old Town and its Square were at the centre of events during every stage in the history of Bohemia.

This view of Prague Castle as seen in the early evening from the Rudolfinum
on náměstí Jana Palacha (Jan Palach Square), leaves one of
the most lasting impressions upon the visitor to Prague

The Old-New Synagogue, erected in around 1270, is the oldest Jewish synagogue still standing in central Europe. Josef Schlesinger carried out the reconstruction of the original Renaissance Jewish Town Hall after 1760

THE JEWISH QUARTER

A detail of the Jewish Town Hall façade — the Star of David with a Swedish army helmet. It was given to the Jews in remembrance of their defence of Prague against the Swedes during the Thirty Years' War

Of all the inhabitants of Prague, it has been the Jews who, since times long past, have occupied the leading position in commerce. There is nothing written of how they came to Bohemia or to neighbouring lands, because this undoubtedly occurred in ancient times. They could, perhaps, already be found in the land during the period of the Markoman tribe, amongst other traders who had arrived from the Roman Empire, and they also moved amongst the Czechs in pagan times, commanding greater respect here . . .

FROM THE BOOK ON THE HISTORY OF PRAGUE
BY VÁCLAV VLADIVOJ TOMEK

The so-called Ceremonial House (Obřadní síň) is suggestive of
a Neo-Romanesque castle. Nowadays it houses
Jewish Museum exhibitions

The Jewish component within the population of mediaeval Prague was marked from the very origins of the town settlement. Alongside Jerusalem, Prague occupied an extraordinary place in Jewish tradition. One legend tells of how the Jews came here after the destruction of the Temple in Jerusalem. However, reliable sources indicate that the Jews began to settle in the area below Prague Castle as early as the 10th century. Jewish traders and immigrants approached Prague — at that time comprising a castle by the river and a number of small markets and trading settlements — from two directions. Those travelling from the Byzantine Empire established themselves in the area around Dušní ulice (Spirit Street) as it is called today. Some time later others arrived in the Old Town from the west and founded their own town, later called the Jewish ghetto. By the 11th and 12th centuries it had already become an unbroken settlement in the area where the Jewish Quarter was subsequently located, roughly between present-day Kaprova ulice and Pařížská leading to the Vltava. When Prague Old Town was formed in the mid-1200s, the status of the Jewish community was altered. It was separated from the Christian part of the town by walls, with gates which were locked at night.

The Jews had their own internal self-government, but as elsewhere in Europe their legal status was regulated by the most diverse decrees and privileges which depended upon whether or not they enjoyed the protection of the monarch. They were considered direct subjects, that is to say the property of the king, who could do as he liked with them; for instance, he could promise to repay his creditors after a further pogrom against his Jewish subjects. The Prague ghetto suffered fewer pogroms in comparison with other countries, but they were carried out with equal cruelty. Diverse circumstances were used as a pretext: the movement of armies fighting in the Crusades, famine in the land, an epidemic or incitement by fanatical preachers.

In spite of the loss of its monopoly on financial affairs and various limitations, the Jewish community won relative peace in the latter half of the 16th century. The Habsburg monarchy was in ever greater need of finance for its wars against the Turks, for representations, for the payment of construction work on the court, and for its political ambitions within the Holy Roman Empire, and thus it was continually obtaining new credits from Jewish bankers and usurers. The leading Jewish banker of the time was Mordechai Maisel, a man of incredible wealth, who often lent considerable sums of money to Emperor Rudolf II. Maisel succeeded in taking full advantage of the situation in order to make life at least a little easier for his fellow believers, obtaining from Rudolf the confirmation of old privileges and the granting of new ones, so as to increase the legal security of Prague's Jews. Maisel was mayor of the Jewish community in the town, and the influence of his extensive building activity is still apparent in the ghetto today. He was responsible for erecting the community's town hall, the current appearance of which dates from the late Baroque era, and the nearby High Synagogue (Vysoká synagóga). He also founded the originally private Maisel Synagogue (Maiselova synagóga), which owes its present appearance to renovation following fire and redevelopment. Visitors are able to admire the permanent exhibition of synagogal silver. Together with his friend, the erudite Rabbi Loew ben Bezallel, this well-known man also established the Talmudic school, and presided over the development of Renaissance science. Loew became a legendary figure in Rudolfine Prague, for he is fabled as the creator of a huge clay figure, something akin to a modern-day robot, called the golem, endowed with fantastic bodily strength. Such strength could be released by the shem, a ball with a magic formula inserted into a hole in the giant's forehead.

Another personality of Renaissance Prague, though in this case a notorious one, was the banker Jakub Bassevi, whose enormous affluence came rather from financial transactions relating to the supply of weapons to the army and from speculation with so-called "lightweight coins" and confiscated possessions, in which he participated with Albrecht Waldstein and various other noblemen and bankers following the defeat of the Estates' uprising.

The tombstones of the aforementioned individuals are situated in the Old Jewish Cemetery (Starý židovský hřbitov), amongst 12,000 others dating from between 1439 and 1787. Together with these are a number of Gothic flat tombstones dating from the 14th century,

At the beginning of the 17th century the Pinkas Synagogue (Pinkasova synagóga) was adapted in the style of the late Renaissance. A ritual bath and well have been preserved in the courtyard

transferred to the cemetery after they were discovered during construction activities on the site of the original Jewish cemetery in the New Town. The Old Jewish Cemetery's oldest plot belongs to Avigdor Kara, and dates back to 1439. Almost fully preserved, this Jewish cemetery is one of the most complete of its kind and is a valuable source of knowledge as far as the history of Prague's Jewish community is concerned.

The entire Jewish population was twice expelled from the country, in 1541 and 1744. Both ill-judged decisions had negative repercussions on trade and financial affairs, which led to their being revoked, under pressure not only from the Jews themselves, but also from the town's burghers, and even its nobility. Likewise on both occasions, the Jewish community reintegrated itself into the economy of Prague and of the country, yet its status did not improve. It was first of all the reforms in keeping with the enlightened absolutism of Joseph II, through which he created the conditions for economic prosperity, which fundamentally influenced life and administration in the ghetto and pulled down the wall of isolation behind which the Jews had been forced to live. Nevertheless, the ten thousand-strong population remained crowded together in the area upon which a number of properties now stand, even though after 1796 Jews were permitted to live in any building in the Old Town. The progressive reform programme of liberalisation, eventually implemented in the 19th century, eliminated practically all isolation. Noticeable differences began to surface within the Jewish community, and many Jews assimilated themselves into the surrounding environment through marriage or merely through everyday coexistence. In most cases they mastered both languages spoken in the country — Czech and German — and thus they sometimes inclined towards Czech circles and sometimes towards the German community. Titles were conferred upon a number of successful businessmen, often after they had converted to Christianity.

As the 19th century came to a close, the Jewish Quarter was in a state of collapse in terms of its social, health and sanitary conditions. Consequently, in the early 1900s the town undertook extensive redevelopment of the mediaeval, Renaissance and Baroque structures in the Jewish Quarter and neighbouring parts of the Old Town. This totally destroyed the character of the old lanes in the Prague ghetto. During the clearance operation many buildings which ought to have been preserved for the next generation were pulled down, along with dilapidated structures. These made way for a new quarter housing eclectic and Art Nouveau buildings containing flats, which in the course of the 20th century have also become important monuments. All that remained of the old ghetto was a handful of properties, for the most part synagogues, and the old town hall. The street network was also partially retained.

The clearance work further accelerated the contemporary process of integrating Prague's Jewish community into cultural, scientific and public life. Their contribution, reflected impressively up until the Second World War in Czech life and in that of the German minority, is symbolised by the names Egon Erwín Kisch, Franz Kafka, Oskar Baum, Max Brod, Eduard Lederer, Vojtěch Rakous, Karel Poláček, Jiří Orten, Egon Hostovský, Rudolf Fuchs and many others.

The advent of Nazism interrupted this thousand year-long symbiosis. Massive emigration ensued, and then the holocaust decimated the remaining Jewish population, namely those who lacked the possibility or the means to abandon their homes, or who were simply reluctant to leave.

After the war few refugees returned to live here permanently, for fear of the future course of events. In the years that followed, the ranks of emigrants were swelled also by many of those who had survived the Nazi atrocities. In the 1950s a large number of Jewish citizens became the victims of false allegations and lawsuits. A great many of them withstood all this, however, and their contribution to the cultural life of Prague and the country as a whole, and to scientific and technological progress, has served merely as a continuation of historical tradition, and far outweighs the current numerical strength of the Jewish community.

The most precious relic of the former mediaeval ghetto is the Old-New Synagogue (Staronová synagóga), one of the oldest Gothic structures in Prague. Dating from circa 1270, the early Gothic building has the look of a two-aisle hall with ribbed vaulting supported on two central pillars. The exterior is adorned with 14th-century brick gable, and below it is sur-

The Old Jewish Cemetery (Starý židovský hřbitov) is one of the Prague's most popular attractions for visitors. Behind this section stands the Klausen Synagogue (Klausová synagóga)

90

Approximately 12,000 tombstones are to be found in the Old Jewish Cemetery.
A great many prominent figures from the Jewish community
in Prague are buried here

rounded by annexes; the northern annexe, for the women, dates from the 18th century. One enters the two-aisle hall through the original portal with early Gothic ornamentation employing plant motifs. Inside the synagogue hangs a banner, a present to the Jews of Prague from Emperor Ferdinand III in recognition of their help in defending the town against the Swedes in the mid-1600s. On the eastern side is the tabernacle

The Klausen Synagogue on U Starého hřbitova (Old Cemetery Street) and the stained glass window with a mosaic of the Star of David

with its Renaissance pillars, above which is the original, early Gothic canopy, filled in with plant foliage on the tympanum.

Situated on the southern edge of the cemetery and Široká is the Pinkas Synagogue (Pinkasova synagóga), founded by Rabbi Pinkas in 1479. It comprises a late Gothic hall, vaulted with a ribbed gable on Renaissance supports. The southern wing and women's gallery, marked on the outside with late Renaissance windows, were added in the early 17th century. The Pinkas Synagogue also contains the Memorial to the Victims of the Holocaust.

The Jewish Town Hall (Židovská radnice), currently home to the Federation of Jewish Religious Communities in Bohemia and Moravia and the Jewish Religious Community in Prague, was created out of the revamp given to Maisel's original town hall, erected by builder Pancras Roder in the late 1500s. The late Baroque remodelling was carried out by the architect Josef Schlesinger in 1763. On the town hall roof stands a wooden turret and a clock with Hebrew figures.

Adjacent to the side of the Town Hall facing Pařížská ulice stands the High Synagogue, also known as the Town Hall Synagogue (Radniční synagóga). The synagogue, the construction of which postdates 1577 and was financed by Mordechai Maisel, underwent extension work in 1691.

The late 17th-century Klausen Synagogue (Klausová synagóga), located on U Starého hřbitova (Old Cemetery Street), was remodelled in the late 1800s. The neighbouring building, erected in 1906, served as the meeting place for the ceremonial brotherhood.

Dušní ulice is home to the Spanish Synagogue (Španělská synagóga), constructed on a design by Adalbert Ignaz Ullman in 1867 and 1868. It owes its name to its Moorish style.

The State Jewish Museum (Státní židovské muzeum), established in 1950, is a significant part of the one time ghetto. (The Prague Jewish Museum was founded back in 1906.) The collections of Jewish artefacts held by the museum, which are open to the public, are the richest in the world.

These monuments, and the activity which once again flourishes in the Jewish Quarter in Prague, create the peculiar atmosphere of a town within a town, which nevertheless is not enclosed by walls. Visitors from all over the world flock here to admire the architecture and museum collections of the Prague ghetto and to honour the memory of past victims of anti-Semitic persecution.

A typical shot of Jewish Prague — Maiselova ulice (Maisel Street), the Old-New Synagogue (Staronová synagóga) and the Jewish Town Hall. A ride through the narrow lanes in a horse-and-carriage is a very popular attraction

The most stunning building in the Lesser Quarter (Malá Strana), the Baroque Church
of St. Nicholas (kostel sv. Mikuláše), is a rewarding subject
for artists and photographers

94

THE LESSER QUARTER

This pretty wax effigy of the Infant Jesus, the *Bambino di Praga*, is of Spanish origin. The *Bambino* can be seen in the Church of Our Lady of Victory (kostel Panny Marie Vítězné) on Karmelitská ulice (Carmelite Street)

On the death of King Wenceslas, his son, the strong and brave Přemysl, ascended the throne of Bohemia. Even in his childhood days he behaved as a man, and everywhere he went he enhanced the nobility of royal courage through the splendour of his gallant deeds. In his endeavours to secure peace for the people of his realm, he set about enclosing the towns with walls and fortifying the castles. Moreover, he fortified the Lesser Town of Prague with walls and moats.

FROM THE CHRONICLE BY FRANCIS OF PRAGUE

The Lesser Quarter (Malá Strana) is one of the most charming areas of Prague. No visitor to Prague ever forgets the breathtaking views afforded from Novotny's Footbridge (Novotného lávka) across the river to the Lesser Quarter bridge tower and the stately dome of the Church of St. Nicholas; to the slim tower rising above the Church of St. Thomas (kostel sv. Tomáše); to the robust Gothic tower of the Church of Our Lady Under the Chain (kostel Panny Marie pod řetězem); to the palaces and gardens climbing upwards towards the castle buildings and the slopes below the Strahov Monastery; or to Petřín Hill and Charles' walls, the lookout tower, and the funicular railway (lanovka) from more recent times.

From the town planner's point of view, the Lesser Quarter is one entity, yet here not only the expert's eye, but also that of the less perceptive passer-by, notices the inseparable and rare symbiosis of various styles. This area of Prague unites the imposing with the intimate, the massive architectural complexes of palaces and churches with the peaceful atmosphere of gardens, lanes and secluded spots. The Lesser Quarter boasts an abundance of natural elements: the Vltava river and its arm, the Devil's Stream (Čertovka), which flows around the greenery on Kampa Island; the flora which grows freely on the extensive slopes of Petřín Hill; and the tended palace gardens. The quarter embodies the spiritual development which began with the advent of the Romanesque period, continued through the Baroque era and ended with the Neoclassical age, as well as the tension between the burghers and the aristocracy, pomp and simplicity, ostentation and practicality. It serves as a reminder of what redevelopment destroyed for ever on the right bank of the Vltava river, and which affected the Lesser Quarter too, though far less dramatically.

The origin and subsequent development of the settlements in the Lesser Quarter are directly linked to Prague Castle. Recent architectural excavations have shown that to discover the origins of modern-day Prague one must look to the left bank of the Vltava beneath the castle. It is precisely this ancient settlement, situated roughly in the area between present-day Malostranské náměstí (Lesser Quarter Square) and the castle, which, in all likelihood, was the first to exist below the castle, together with a market-place. To its advantage it was located by the river, though far enough away to escape flooding, and above all it lay on the main route taken for long-distance journeys which, after crossing a ford in the Vltava, thanks to the shallow course of the river, proceeded approximately through the area occupied today by Nerudova (Neruda Street) and Úvoz upwards and to the west.

In the area that was to become the Lesser Quarter, however, lay a number of communities and villages which later partially vanished or were incorporated into the main body of the future town. Since it grew up naturally in line with developments in communications and the relief of the terrain, by the end of the Romanesque period the Lesser Quarter had still not evolved into one single community, and began to develop at a quicker pace especially in the 12th century.

The reign of King Vladislav I was a significant one with regard to the further expansion of Prague. It was during this period that the rôle of the market on Prague's right bank increased greatly, and when the wooden bridge over the Vltava collapsed during a flood, the king commissionned an unknown Italian builder, perhaps from Milan, to erect a new, stone bridge between 1158 and 1172 in honour of his consort, Judith. Spanning the Vltava with a yellow sandstone bridge able to withstand heavy traffic brought the settlements on either side of the river and both castles closer together. The Judith Bridge and the bridge over the Danube at Regensburg were the only ones of their kind in central Europe to be built in stone, and the former was rightly described by the chronicler as the emperor's work. The bridge remained in use until 1342, when it too was destroyed in a flood, and a new bridge replaced it in the reign of Charles IV.

In 1158 the second King Vladislav of Bohemia assigned a large site to the left of the Lesser Quarter end of the bridge, probably defended by two Romanesque towers guarding the gate, to the Knights of the Order of St. John for the construction of a complex and the Church of Our Lady Under the Chain. In approximately 1270 a new Gothic sanctuary was added to the church. The complex enjoyed its own jurisdiction, and as a separate independent entity it was also fortified. In the second half of the 14th century, during Charles IV's reign, the church underwent considerable reconstruction, and other properties in the

A number of old houses and palaces line the Romanesque Castle Steps
(Zámecké schody) linking the Lesser Quarter
with Prague Castle

The dome on the Church of St. Nicholas in the Lesser Quarter forms
the background of the view of a section of the Leslie Thun
Palace, currently home to the British Embassy

Order's grounds were remodelled. The Parler-style narthex in the church and the two huge Gothic towers recall the important status of the Order in Bohemia and of its Prague seat.

To the north of the area leading up to the bridge in the Lesser Quarter another large space was created, namely the Bishop's Court. The splendid buildings and extensive garden are a legacy first and foremost of the last Bishop of Prague, John IV of Dražice, who spent many years of his life at the papal court at Avignon. On his return he ordered the rebuilding of the as yet unimpressive Romanesque residence in Gothic style. However, during the battle for the Lesser Quarter in the initial stages of the Hussite Revolution, the palace and the adjoining garden were burnt down and destroyed. All that remains of the entire structure today is the massive, prismatic, early Gothic tower, which bears the coat of arms of the nobles of Dražice above the entrance.

Let us, however, return to the first half of the 13th century. Although without doubt the Romanesque community below Prague Castle had urban characteristics and was already at least partly fortified, it was a disjointed, scattered settlement which evaded the king's rigid control. The monarch was doubtless interested in firmly securing the area leading up to the bridge, through which passed the important communication route joining the castle with the bridge. Towards the end of his reign, in 1253, Wenceslas I had the area before the Judith Bridge in the Lesser Quarter reinforced with walls and ramparts attached to the Bishop's Court and the Monastery of St. John. A mere four years later, his son, Přemysl Otakar II, founded the town as a whole to replace, for strategic reasons, the uneven settlement situated between the castle and the stone bridge. On his orders it was fortified on three sides by a wall and a moat; only on the side next to the castle was no wall built. The town received the name New Town Below Prague Castle, and was opened up predominantly to German colonists. (When Charles IV subsequently established the New Town on the right bank of the Vltava in 1348, the New Town Below Prague Castle became known as the Lesser Town, and later as the Lesser Quarter.) The Parish Church of St. Nicholas, in the middle of Malostranské náměstí, the predecessor to the existing Baroque church which still stands today, was consecrated by Bishop Tobias in 1283, and at about the same time the sizeable Augustinian Friary at the Church of St. Thomas came into existence.

Charles IV enlarged substantially the territory occupied by the Lesser Quarter by adding to it the wide space along the river to the south of the St. John complex and the eastern slopes of Petřín Hill. This entire area was encircled by the so-called Hunger Wall (Hladová zeď), from 1360—1362, which ran from the southwestern corner of the Hradčany fortifications, continued on to the western edge of the Strahov Monastery and the Church of St. Lawrence on Petřín Hill (kostel sv. Vavřince na Petříně), and then eastwards to the river. The clay slate wall stands some six metres high and is nearly two metres thick. The new fortifications joined the Lesser Quarter with the territory containing the St. John complex and a large part of Újezd village, Nebovidy village and Strahov.

When the Hussite Wars broke out in November 1419 the Lesser Quarter suffered heavily in the battles fought between the citizens of Prague, who held the Lesser Quarter bridge towers and the nearby house of the Dukes of Saxony, and the sizeable garrison of the united nobility supporting the claim of Sigismund, King of Hungary and Rome, to the throne of Bohemia. In the course of the fighting, the Archbishop's Palace (Mostecká Street) at the entry into the Lesser Quarter from the bridge was burnt to the ground, as were the buildings situated beneath the castle and the churches in the Lesser Quarter. The town hall in the middle of the square was destroyed. In the spring of 1420, when the town's inhabitants were preparing to brave a siege by the army fighting in the Crusades, practically every building from the Hussite-held area on the Lesser Quarter side of the bridge to the castle was set ablaze and razed to the ground so that it might not be used in any secret attempt to penetrate Hussite positions. Even the trees in the Archbishop's Palace garden were cut down so as to prevent any unobserved approach towards the Hussite defences.

It was not until George of Poděbrady ascended the throne in the mid-15th century that the Lesser Quarter began to recover from the hardships it had experienced. In 1464 the first stone of the new northern Lesser Quarter bridge tower was laid. Today both to-

99

The houses and small palaces of the Lesser Quarter
climb up the slope as far as the palaces
of Prague Castle

wers—the original, smaller Romanesque tower and its more recent, late Gothic counterpart — still guard the approach from the bridge to Mostecká ulice (Bridge Street) in the Lesser Quarter.

With the advent of the Renaissance, the Lesser Quarter began to bloom into unprecedented beauty; until, that is, on 2 July 1541, fire swept through a house called On The Rampart (Na Baště) on Malostranské náměstí. Fanned by a strong wind, the flames spread swiftly, engulfing the surrounding shingle-roofed buildings and the friary of St. Thomas, and setting alight both sides of present-day Nerudova. The blaze destroyed the buildings below the castle, and even spread as far as Hradčany and the castle itself. Within three hours two-thirds of the Lesser Quarter had vanished; 133 of its 211 properties had been set on fire.

The fire constituted the basic reason why instead of carrying out complex remodelling, so-called "green turf" construction was begun in many areas, both on the original sites of property once owned by burghers and on large parcels of land. The purchases were made for the most part by the aristocracy, from burghers rendered impoverished in the aftermath of the fire. Many former burgher-owned buildings therefore made way for Renaissance town houses boasting spacious courtyards and gardens.

Although thus far Renaissance-style elements had been somewhat slow in penetrating Prague, this new architectural style now showed through strongly in the rebuilding of larger property for the aristocracy on the sites destroyed by the blaze. Together with the persecution suffered by the burghers' Estate after Ferdinand I quelled the 1547 uprising, this nobility-led reconstruction drive served to weaken the influence of the Lesser Quarter burghers in the administration of their town. Furthermore, the nobility undertaking this reconstruction work invoked its

A pretty house sign adorns The Three Little Fiddles (U Tří housliček) on Nerudova (Neruda Street). It recalls the fact that between 1667 and 1748 the house belonged by turns to three generations of Prague violin-makers

101

right to enter their property into the so-called Land Records, an ancient institution dating back to the latter half of the 13th century, consisting of the archives of legal decrees, agreements and property transactions by those included in the records, that is to say the nobles themselves. Property listed in the records was not subject to the towns' jurisdiction, whereby the status of self-government for the burghers was undermined still further.

Building activities also provoked demographic changes. Prague witnessed the arrival of members of the building profession from all over Bohemia. Moreover, an increase was registered in the number of builders, masons, plasterers and other craftsmen arriving from Italy and German-speaking countries. A sizeable Italian community grew up within the Lesser Quarter, gradually establishing its own hospital, chapel and cemetery.

A further increase in building activity and a high level of immigration characterised the last two decades of the 16th century, when Emperor Rudolf II established his court in Prague. A flurry of construction work took place, as elsewhere, in the area between the bridge and U Lužického semináře and Míšeňská ulice (Lusatian Seminary Street and Meissen Street). Painstaking Renaissance-style restoration work was carried out on the Church of St. Thomas following the fires of 1503 and 1541. A number of Renaissance houses sprang up on Tomášská ulice (Thomas Street), Valdštejnská ulice (Waldstein Street) and Letenská ulice (Letná Street), and the same style was applied to the adaptation of the majority of structures in the Lesser Quarter.

Trade and craftsmanship recovered, and the interest displayed by the aristocracy in building town houses increased further, as illustrated by the splendid Hradec family palace, the Renaissance gables of which inspire admiration to this day. In addition, construction of the large Smiřický Palace (palác Smiřických) for that important and rich noble family was commenced on Malostranské náměstí; new, Renaissance houses were erected on Mostecká; and the Judith Tower at the end of the bridge was restored by means of the removal of its battlements, the substitution of gables and a roof, and the addition of *sgraffito* plaster. Of the extensive Renaissance buildings erected by the Mettychs of Čečov, only Breitschwert House on Velkopřevorské náměstí (Grand Prior's Square) has been preserved.

The late Renaissance period brought development to the town, as demonstrated by the revamping (1617—1622) of the Lesser Quarter Town Hall (Malostranská radnice), originally the home of Jan Tovačovský of Cimburk, by Giovanni Campione de Bossi, on a design by Giovanni Maria Filippi. The town hall stands on Malostranské náměstí opposite the Church of St. Thomas. Only the shell of the original structure can be seen today, as the gables and towers which initially adorned it were removed in the early 1800s.

As was the case elsewhere in Prague and the country as a whole, in the late 16th and early 17th centuries work on religious buildings stagnated to a certain extent. Any new construction activity mirrored changes in the religious habits of the town population. The German Lutherans, who settled in the Lesser Quarter, erected their own church on Karmelitská ulice (Carmelite Street) in 1611, and likewise their fellow believers built the Church of the Holy Saviour in the Old Town. After 1624, as the recatholicisation of the country began, the church in the Lesser Quarter was given to the Carmelites. The church's altar originally faced east, in keeping with tradition, but during early Baroque remodelling in the 1630s the sanctuary was moved and a tower and façade erected. The Church of Our Lady of Victory is famous throughout the world for its 16th-century wax effigy of the Infant Jesus, the *Bambino di Praga,* which Polyxena of Lobkowicz brought from Spain and gave to the Carmelites in 1628.

In the same way as the German Lutherans in the Lesser Quarter, the Italian community there added to their hospital in present-day Vlašská ulice (Italy Street) their own, naturally Catholic, Church of St. Carlo Borromeo. Its Old Town counterpart became the Church of the Assumption (kostel Nanebevzetí Panny Marie), now situated in Karlova, adjacent to the Clementinum's Jesuit college.

The 17th century brought with it a chain of woes and hardship to the towns of Prague, and especially to Hradčany and the Lesser Quarter. First of all, in February 1611 they were both occupied and plundered by the mercenary troops of Archduke Leopold, Bishop of Passau, invited into the country by Rudolf II in his attempt to turn the

102

The main altar in the Church of St. Joseph dates from the late 17th century. The painting
of the Holy Family is the work of the distinguished
Czech artist, Petr Brandl

103

tide in his relations with the rebellious Czech Estates and his own brother, Emperor Matthias, who coveted the Bohemian throne.

Further pillage of the Lesser Quarter—during which the houses belonging to the aristocracy were particularly badly affected — came at the hands of the armies aligned with the Catholic League and the Emperor, which entered Prague after the Battle of White Mountain. The town had been left to its fate when Frederick of the Palatinate fled. Confiscations and the emigration of non-Catholics ensued, and the Lesser Quarter became greatly depopulated.

When Prague was later occupied for a time by troops under the command of Hans von Arnim, the Lesser Quarter and the other Prague towns found themselves forced to withstand yet more in-

justice, on this occasion at the hands of mercenaries loyal to the Lutheran Elector of Saxony.

Swedish troops penetrated the Lesser Quarter in 1648. Thanks to the bravery displayed by their defenders, the Old and New Towns managed to keep the invaders out, but the castle, Hradčany and the Lesser Quarter were totally ransacked. This accounts for the erection of new fortifications based on the latest developments in military science at the time, undertaken shortly after the Thirty Years' War came to a close, and which continued into the 18th century. The Baroque fortifications replaced their original mediaeval predecessors, and blocked enemy access to the town.

Few individuals were able to cope with the unfavourable conditions created by the Thirty Years' War.

The Baroque building bearing the name The Painters' House (U Malířů) now houses a wine restaurant boasting delicious cuisine

104

The Fürstenberg Palace (Fürstenberský palác), dating from 1743—1747, is one of the architectural gems in Valdštejnská ulice (Waldstein Street) in the Lesser Quarter, and boasts glorious and specious gardens

105

The Lesser Quarter provides many romantic and tranquil settings, such
as U Lužického semináře (Lusatian Seminary Street)
with its pastel façades

Objects of interest in Prague include its water mills. The mill on the Devil's Stream, with its remarkable wooden mill-wheel, is called the Grand Prior's Mill (Velkopřevorský mlýn)

The Baroque Buquoy Palace (Buquoyský palác) on Velkopřevorské
náměstí (Grand Prior's Square), now
the French Embassy

108

However, one of those able to do so was General Albrecht Waldstein, later Duke of Friedland. He was rewarded to an amazing extent both by his advantageous marriage and conversion to Catholicism, and by his timely switch to the Habsburg camp. He exploited his position excellently, profiting unscrupulously from the confiscations that followed the Battle of White Mountain, and participating in the dubious but lucrative speculative deals undertaken by a banking consortium which he headed. Yet most of all it was the incredible economic power that he amassed which allowed him to clothe, arm and feed his entire army from his own pocket. The Duke accumulated property on a massive scale, and became the richest, most powerful and most influential man in the realm, ahead of the emperor himself, who was often little more than the crowned servant of Waldstein's military undertakings.

Between 1624 and 1630 Waldstein commissioned the construction of a huge palace complex the size of an urban district or small town on the site occupied at the time by twenty-three houses, three gardens and the municipal brick kiln, all or which he purchased for the purpose. Giovanni Pieroni designed the palace, which was erected by Andrea Spezza and Niccolò Sebregondi; they also worked on the Duke's other building projects outside Prague. Extraordinary care was employed in fitting out the massive complex with rare furniture, tapestries, carpets, paintings, statues and tableware.

When Albrecht Waldstein was murdered in the western Bohemian town of Cheb in 1634, the directory listing confiscated palace property filled a number of pages, and constitutes a valuable source of insight into how the splendid residence of this Renaissance magnate might have looked, its luxurious nature surpassing that of many a royal residence of the period. The paintings by Baccio Bianco which decorate the ceiling of the Hall of Knights represent Waldstein as the God Mars, and the magnificent terrace, or sala terrena, which leads into the garden — or rather into grounds comprising several gardens — is magnificent. Everything here testifies to the Duke's self-confidence and taste. The array of sculptures in the garden, predating 1630, were the creation of Adriaen de Vries, who had previously been sculptor to the court of Rudolf II. A collection of casts from several of the figures is now situated in the garden; the original sculptures were removed to Drottningholm Palace by the Swedes as war spoils.

Although the Waldstein Palace (Valdštejnský palác) caused little upheaval in the art forms employed in the Lesser Quarter, it is true to say that it influenced town planning considerably and initiated the transformation of the area into a part of Prague containing stunning palaces and gardens.

In spite of the negative consequences of the revolt by the Estates and wars, the curtailing of the Estates' rights, and Prague's relegation to the rôle of playing second fiddle to Vienna, the building of palaces for the noblesse continued apace, and was especially strong in the late 17th century and the 18th century. Generals, colonels and lower-ranked officers in the imperial army, members of the remaining domestic Catholic families, and many recent converts, all took part in this construction drive. The Renaissance Vchynský Palace was bought by Pavel Michna of Vacínov after 1624, but it was in essence his son Václav who turned the existing structure into a beautiful Baroque palace, the interior of which was decorated by the plasterer Domenico Galli. The remodelling of Michna Palace (Michnův palác), executed according to a design by Francesco Caratti, was overseen by Pietro Colombo, and completed only in the first half of the 18th century, when Duke Schwarzenberg bought the building.

The palace gardens underneath Prague Castle make for a splendid sight. Only the large Fürstenberg Palace enjoyed such an advantageous location as to make it possible when laying out its gardens to combine the flat parterre with an impressive background of terraces. The sites housing the remaining palaces climbing up the steep castle slope were considerably narrower, and thus they were cleverly divided into a system of terraces, steps and arbours, combining the intimacy of the private gardens with extensive views of the town.

The Baroque and Rococo palaces, such as the Nostitz, Thun, Buquoy, Kaiserstein, Vrtba, Morzin, Schönborn, Grand Prior's, Liechtenstein, Lobkowicz, Ledebour, Turba, Kounic and Palffy Palaces, and others, with their rich and often lavish relief decoration, changed the entire face and character of the Lesser Quarter. On its southern side along the Vltava and on Kampa Island past the Devil's Stream, an arm of the river, and indeed on the other side leading onto the slopes of Petřín Hill and below the castle, it was possible to extend these residences and encircle them with the many gardens which to this day provide an element of greenery. The Lesser Quarter became a peaceful, sizeable and nostalgic secluded spot in Prague which embraced modern times at a very slow rate. An exception to this was the Thun Palace, situated in Sněmovní ulice (Assembly Street) as it is known today. The Provincial Assembly, originally the supreme body of the community of Estates, met here in the second half of the 19th century as the country's elected parliamentary body during the establishment of a constitutional monarchy, until 1918, and the birth of the Czechoslovak Republic, when the Assembly became the seat of the National Assembly's Senate. Currently it is often used by the Parliament of the Czech Republic. The inscription "Salus Rei Publicae Suprema Lex Esto" ("The Health of the State Is the Supreme Law") completes the decoration of the tympanum in the centre of the palace façade.

A small economic boom allowed the middle class to follow the aristocracy's lead in embarking upon building work. Despite subsequent alterations, the buildings, erected for the most part for the middle class, on what are now Dražického náměstí (Dražický Square), Míšeňská, U Lužického semináře, Na Kampě (Kampa Street), Prokopská ulice (Prokop Street), Lázeňská ulice (Bath Street) and Mostecká, retained their interesting character. After 1700 the squares and streets of the Lesser Quarter, beginning at the centre, acquired their Baroque, and subsequently Rococo and Neoclassical appearance. In many a place, however, the façade merely conceals the older work, which is not only apparent in the internal structural layouts, but was also a telling factor in defining the plans elaborated for façades.

With the advent of re-catholicisation, the construction of religious buildings enjoyed a revival, stimulated above all by the Orders — both the old, established communities returning to the realm, and others arriving in the country for the first time. The most energetic of all were the Jesuits, who in 1628 settled at the Parish Church of St. Nicholas in the middle of Malostranské náměstí and adjacent to it, on top of existing structures, erected a huge college complex between 1672 and 1687, splitting the as then continuous square into two parts. In the early 1700s an imposing new church relaced the original Gothic structure. Kristof Dienzenhofer worked on the remarkable vaulted nave between 1701 and 1711, and his son, Kilian Ignaz, built the presbytery with its massive dome between 1737 and 1752. A tall bell tower, erected by Anselmo Lurago from 1751 to 1756, brought the construction of the complex as a whole to completion. The church's façade and its massive entrance face onto the upper part of the original small square opposite the Liechtenstein Palace. Its interior constitutes one of the greatest accomplishments of the Prague Baroque, succeeding in naturally combining architecture, sculptures and paintings in a fantastic whole. Four colossal statues of the Doctors of the Church by Ignaz Platzer constitute a dominant feature. The painting in the dome is the work of Franz Xavier Balko. Here the creators of the church furthermore succeeded in converting a magnificent idea into a reality in absolute harmony with the whole, and thus in spite of its being such a dominant feature, the structure blends in with its surroundings.

A second masterpiece of sacred Baroque architecture in the Lesser Quarter is the monastic church of St. Thomas, the origins of which date back to the latter half of the 13th century. The building was devastated by fires in 1419 and 1541, re-emerging in a remodelled state on each occasion. The basic tall, three-aisle structure was not destroyed, however, and it remained untouched by the Baroque architect Kilian Ignaz Dienzenhofer's adaptations between 1724 and 1731. Václav Reiner decorated the newly-erected arches with stunning frescoes, which rank amongst some of the Lesser Quarter's leading artistic work. Besides the rich decoration, the church boasts a remarkable collection of furniture and art work from the original decoration, showing how the Prague Baroque developed. Several of the unique works date back as far as the Rudolfine period.

Above the early-18th-century Thun-Hohenstein Palace (currently home to the Italian Embassy) on Nerudova stands the Church of Our Lady of

The huge façade, dome and tower of the Church of St. Nicholas
in the Lesser Quarter stand out in the magical
night-time illumination

111

The autumnal shades of Petřín Hill. The viewing tower, standing sixty metres high, was erected as an imitation of the Eiffel Tower and is a famous Prague landmark

Providence (kostel Panny Marie Božské prozřetelnosti), erected by the Theatine Order between 1691 and 1717. Leading Prague Baroque builders Jean-Baptiste Mathey and Giovanni Santini-Aichl worked on the construction of the church. The steps between the palace and the church take one from Nerudova ulice to the Castle Steps beneath the castle, laid in the late 1500s during the reign of Maximilian II.

An example of the encounter between the various structural styles in the Lesser Quarter is the Carmelite Church of St. Joseph (kostel sv. Josefa), dating from 1687—93, and probably erected on a Dutch Baroque design by an architect and member of the Order, Johann Raas. Its façade is divided up by half-columns and pilasters with circular bosses and adorned with statues by Matthias Jäckel. The paintings of the Holy Family and St. Theresa inside the church, dating from the early 1700s, are the work of the leading Czech painter of the Prague Baroque, Petr Brandl.

Whilst the Thirty Years' War was still being fought, thanks to the Grand Prior Duke Rudolf Colloredo-Waldsee and Prior Bernard de Witt, the Knights of the Order of St. John (the Knights of Malta) commenced renovation work on their seat. The monastic Church of Our Lady Under the Chain, in essence consisting merely of a sanctuary preserved from the mediaeval church and remodelled in Baroque style by Carlo Lurago in the mid-17th century, was transformed into an intimate space, carefully made complete with quality decoration and furniture. The main altar painting of the Battle of Lepanto and of the member of the Maltese Order in adoration of the Madonna, and the painting of the Beheading of St. Barbara at the side altar, are works by Karel Škréta from the mid-1600s. In the 1700s the monastery and Grand Prior's Palace (Velkopřevorský palác) were added to either side of the church.

Although serious plans to this effect existed, the Lesser Quarter was spared the radical redevelopment carried out on the right bank of the Vltava in the course of the 19th and 20th centuries. At the Pod Petřínem Hospital the late Neoclassical Church of St. Carlo Borromeo was erected in 1855 for the community of the Sisters of Charity. In addition to this the Lesser Quarter also saw the construction of several more important buildings and houses for the middle class in Neoclassical styles, chiefly in the area approachning Újezd. Reaching the top of Petřín Hill was facilitated by the installation of a funicular railway in 1891 to mark Prague's Jubilee Exhibition held that year. The same occasion was celebrated by the erection of a viewing tower, a sixty metre-high miniature model of the Eiffel Tower. A visit to the nearby Church of St. Lawrence is one the visitor will not forget. Standing near to the town walls, the structure was originally founded in the Romanesque period and acquired its current Baroque appearance on the basis of a design by Kilian Ignaz Dienzenhofer, paid for by the Guild of Prague Chefs. Of equal interest is the so-called Maze, situated opposite. Its mirrored passage re-enacts for the visitor a battle between the citizens of Prague and the Swedish on the Charles Bridge in 1648.

Yet a visit to the sights of the Lesser Quarter by no means ends there, for every house, palace and garden, secluded spot or lane has its own history, written by its owner, creator or inhabitant. On leaving Malostranské náměstí, whether by taking the tram or metro or by walking through a lane, the visitor will always find a house, palace or view worthy of admiration.

113

The exterior and interior decoration of the National Theatre (Národní divadlo)
is the boast of late-19th century Czech art. However, this huge
sculpture, Triga, dates from the early 20th century

114

PRAGUE NEW TOWN

The National Theatre, under the motto Národ sobě (A Nation for Itself), was erected in the style of the late Northern Italian Renaissance between 1868 and 1881. The Czech architect Josef Zítek drew up the plans for the theatre. Its artistic decoration is the work of a generation of National Theatre artists

On St. Mark's Day, in the year of our Lord 1348, Charles, King of Rome and Bohemia, laid the foundation stone establishing Prague New Town, and gave orders that the strongest walls with gateways and extremely high towers be erected from Vyšehrad to Poříčí. He also instructed that gardens and vineyards be planted around the town of Prague, and because of such gardens and vineyards the population increased considerably.

BENEŠ KRABICE OF WEITMILE
CHRONICLE OF A PRAGUE CHURCH

The imposing façade of the National Museum, a dominant feature of Wenceslas Square.
It was erected according to plans elaborated by architect Josef Schulz
in Neo-Renaissance style between 1885 and 1890

The most important area of the National Museum is the pantheon, a national
temple dedicated to the memory of the Czech Nation's
great personalities

The Ursuline Convent and Church of St. Ursula, together with the National Theatre complex, are the most striking features of the section of Národní třída (National Avenue) nearest the Vltava river embankment

118

This corner house, erected in 1905, is the first in a line of interesting
early-20th century buildings on Masarykovo
nábřeží (Masaryk Embankment)

119

The Sylva-Taroucca Palace, constructed on the basis of plans by Prague Baroque
architect Kilian Ignag Dientzenhofer, is one the most important buildings
on the busy street called Na Příkopě (On the Moat)

An area beyond the Old Town walls, in the wide bend between Vyšehrad to the south and the river bank opposite Štvanice Island to the north, was demarcated for a new town district. The walls of Prague New Town, extending for nearly three and a half kilometres, were erected within two years, and to the south met the Vyšehrad fortress above the river Botič. Taking the preserved sections of the New Town walls above the Nusle valley as a yardstick, it is possible to state that the town wall was some two or three metres thick and as many as six metres high, with a walkway for its defenders. A moat and a rampart protected the simple structure, which had no auxiliary wall. Two large corner walls—one at Karlov (Charles Quarter) above the Botič valley, and the other at the southeast end of the walls opposite Vítkov hill — served to strengthen the wall, along with a line of nineteen towers and three gates on the route between two towers and a fortified gate, the so-called St. John's Gate, Blind Gate, or Gate of Swine. Where it met the Old Town and Vyšehrad, however, the New Town was not fully enclosed, and the riverside area of the newly-founded town extending from Podskalí, at the confluence of the Botič and Vltava rivers, to St. Wenceslas' Rock at Zderaz, also remained unfortified. That rock was the site upon which Charles' son, Wenceslas IV, subsequently had a small castle erected to guard the river bank. From there northwards as far as the Old Town walls, free access by river to the unfortified bank of the town was made difficult by a system of weirs, a practically insurmountable obstacle. The lower New Town along the river was not protected by walls either, but again crossing the river was hard for the enemy, precisely because of the weirs, which extended as far as the place where the stretch of wall met the Vltava, and because in any case reaching the river on the opposite side was no simple task, owing to the steep slopes at Letná.

It is not known which architect drew up the urban development plans for the New Town, yet the political and cultural stamp of Charles IV is very much discernible. His concept of a town befitting the rôle played by the king of Rome and corresponding to the importance of the Holy Roman Empire had been formed earlier in the more developed environments of France and northern Italy, with which he had acquainted himself as a young prince. It is, therefore, understandable that the existing town of Prague, its size and its architectural richness, still far from satisfied Charles' requirements for a royal town fit for the most powerful ruler in Christendom at that time.

Charles' notion of town planning for the new municipal district envisaged building upon and populating a vast area with a large number of squares, streets, churches and monasteries worthy of comparison with the large towns he had had the opportunity to see in his youth. An overall site measuring 360 hectares was marked out and divided up. Three central areas, to which a network of streets and lanes was joined, formed the basic focal points of the town: the cattle market, now Karlovo náměstí (Charles Square), which with a surface area exceeding eight hectares was Europe's largest square of the period; the horse market, or Wenceslas Square (Václavské náměstí) as it is known today, more than four hectares in size; and the hay market, now Senovážné náměstí (Hay Square), the main square of the lower part of the town, acting as a hay and cereals market.

Prague New Town was to adhere to the same legal statutes as the Old Town and have an independent town council. Each recipient of a parcel of land had one month in which to commence building activities, and these should be completed within eighteen months. Mortgages on town houses were restricted to a maximum of fifty per cent of the building's value, so that proprietors should always be in a position to carry out the necessary maintenance. Charles also included a provision in his foundation charter, according special protection to the Jewish population.

The enclosure of the original town settlements and their parish churches, together with the establishment of other parishes around new churches, led to the eventual division of the New Town into twelve parish districts, and in addition to these the monarch created more churches and monasteries. The Church of St. Apollinarius (kostel sv. Apolináře) was erected after 1362 on the Hill of Winds (Větrná hora) in the upper part of the town, not far from the site upon which Charles had founded an Augustinian convent and the Church of St. Catherine (kostel sv. Kateřiny) in 1354. Of the original church there remains only a slim tower, the highest levels of which are octagonal in shape. Its appearance has earned it the title of the Prague Minaret. The Benedictine Order was installed in the new large Abbey of the Slavs (klášter Na Slovanech), or Emmaus Monastery (klášter Emauzy), with its Church

121

The dome-shaped, richly decorated foyer of the Main Station (Hlavní nádraží) in the
town centre, constructed in Art Nouveau style on a design by architect
Josef Fanta in the early 20th century

Lady and the Slavonic Patron Saints (kostel Panny Marie a slovanských patronů). The monks followed the Old Slavonic liturgy, recalling the ancient tradition of Cyril and Methodius and the rôle played by the Church in converting Moravia and Bohemia to Christianity. Construction of the entire complex was initiated in 1348 and was formally consecrated in 1372. The monastic Church of the Assumption and Charlemagne (kostel Nanebevzetí Panny Marie a sv. Karla Velikého), also built at this time, on the highest site of the New Town, above the Botič river valley facing Vyšehrad, belonged to the Augustinians, and merely confirms the affinity of Charles IV for Charlemagne, whom he described as his predecessor and model ruler.

The additional monasteries founded by Charles IV stood as a testament to the monarch's efforts at achieving integration, for at his request the majority of them were allocated to recently-arrived orders. For instance, in the Botič valley below Vyšehrad, not far from the New Town fortifications, the Servite Order was granted its own monastery and small Church of the Annunciation (kostel Zvěstování Panny Marie), erected after

1360. Near the New Town moat, the massive Church of Our Lady of the Snows (kostel Panny Marie Sněžné), belonging to the Carmelites, and the Church of St. Ambrose (kostel sv. Ambrože) with the monastery of the Benedictines of the Milanese rite, were erected. The latter building was situated on a site opposite to where the Powder Tower currently stands.

The foundation of the New Town also led to the reconstruction of the old Dominican Church of St. Clement's (kostel sv. Klimenta) in Petrská čtvrť (Peter Quarter), completed some time towards the end of Charles' reign. Remodelling also altered the Peter Quarter Parish Church of St. Peter (kostel sv. Petra) at Poříčí and churches in Jircháře. The Church of St. Wenceslas in Zderaz (kostel sv. Václava na Zderaze) was constructed, but the district's monastery had collapsed into ruin by the beginning of the Hussite Revolution.

One of the first structures on which work was begun in the New Town was the Parish Church of SS Henry and Kunhuta (kostel sv. Jindřicha a Kunhuty) in the vicinity of the hay market, followed shortly after, in 1350, by the Parish Church of St. Stephen (kostel

The sculptural and stucco ornamentation on Prague's Main Station is another excellent sample of pure Prague Art Nouveau architecture

The Hotel Evropa, with its stunning façade, is situated on Wenceslas Square. The architects of this superb Art Nouveau building were Bedřich Bendelmayer and Alois Dryák

123

Typical decoration on the façade of an Art Nouveau building on Masarykovo nábřeží,
showing the expressive sculpture of the figure of a young girl, ornamental mascarons
in the form of human faces, and stucco branches around the entrance

sv. Štěpána). All these sacred buildings together show how religious architecture was born and spread through the New Town in Charles' time. The feature common to all the churches constructed in the New Town in the reign of Charles was the tendency to create a harmonious interior and make the external dimensions fit in with existing and envisaged structures.

On the first Friday after Easter Day in every year of Emperor Charles IV's reign, in the middle of the cattle market (now Karlovo náměstí), the imperial relics were displayed. The *reliquiae imperiales* were kept initially in St. Vitus' Cathedral, before being transferred to Karlštejn Castle. A large wooden structure, a tower of some kind, from which they were exhibited, was erected for the occasion. In the reign of Charles' son, Wenceslas IV, a Chapel of the Holy Sacrament was built on the same spot between 1387 and 1393.

By the issuance of a special deed, Charles gave an undertaking to the inhabitants of the Old Town to the effect that the foundation of the New Town would be in no way detrimental to them. He guaranteed them free passage through the town and entrusted to them the defence of the two New Town gates. He did, nonetheless, order certain crafts, which had become a burden to the crowded and overpopulated Old Town through their noise or odours, to move into the New Town. The monarch attempted furthermore to unite the towns of Prague, and for a time (1367—1377) his efforts were realised; however, the imbalance in the status of the communities, together with the mutual acrimony existing between its citizens, compelled him to restore the status quo.

The birth and development of the New Town changed the composition of the population of mediaeval Prague. Whilst the balance of power in the Old Town was tilted in favour of the merchant patricians, craftsmen of Czech origin dominated the New Town, even though a section of the Old Town inhabitants, attracted by the advantages of, and prospects for future economic development, moved there, and new inhabitants from abroad came to settle in the New Town, too.

The ethnic, religious and social conditions existing in the New Town defined it as the place where the Hussite movement acquired its radical nature in its early stages. Prague's first defenestration took place in the New Town at the end of July 1419, under the leadership of the former Premonstratensian priest, Jan Želivský, a Hussite preacher at the Church of Our Lady of the Snows, an event in which Jan Žižka of Trocnov, destined to become a famous personality, participated. When negotiations between Jan Želivský and the detested anti-Hussite councillors appointed by King Wenceslas IV to administer the New Town regarding the release of imprisoned Hussite leaders failed to yield any result, a crowd of Hussite supporters invaded the New Town Hall (Novoměstská radnice) and hurled all the councillors present out of the town hall windows onto the lances and halberds awaiting them below. As the Hussite chronicler records, "this deed struck fear into the enemy of truth in Prague". In view of the fact that the Utraquists dominated the Old Town Hall, the whole of Prague appeared to be in Hussite hands. Hence Wenceslas IV had no alternative but to sanction the new councillors elected by the revolutionary group.

So the rebellion in the New Town marked the commencement of the Hussite Revolution, in which the New Town maintained a consistently more radical stance than its older, richer neighbour, Prague Old Town. It leant upon its alliance with Jan Žižka and his followers, and, after the leader's death, with his successors, who dubbed themselves the orphans.

However, the mutual rivalry between the two Hussite towns constantly came to the fore whenever the need to repulse the common enemy abated, and the help of Hussite Prague's provincial allies was then required to iron out these differences. The antagonism reached its peak on the eve of the Battle of Lipany in May 1434, when the Old Town, supported by troops loyal to the League of Nobles, inflicted a humiliating military defeat on their permanent rival and revoked the privileges enjoyed by the New Town Hall.

The so-called Compacts of Basle, through which the Hussites obtained official recognition of their fundamental dogmatic claims, guaranteed, *inter alia*, equal rights for Utraquists and Catholics. This notwithstanding, the burghers in the Prague towns placed a condition on obtaining citizenship, namely the religious right to receive communion in both kinds. The stone tablet on which the articles of the Compacts were inscribed was placed on a wall in the Chapel of the Holy Sacrament in the New Town's largest marketplace and, moreover, the place in which the Hussite Revolution began, thus symbolically announcing the victory of the

Prague New Town. On the left, the imposing National Theatre building;
on the right, on Masarykovo nábřeží (Masaryk Embankment),
stunning Art Nouveau and pseudo-historical buildings

127

The extraordinary decoration on the portal of an Art Nouveau
building on Masarykovo nábřeží, the headquarters of
the Hlahol patriotic choral society

Revolution. The Hussites' archenemy, Sigismund of Luxemburg, was finally recognised as sovereign of Bohemia only with their consent. New Town citizens also formed part of the delegations sent to Brno and Jihlava to formulate the conditions for Sigismund's accession to the throne, and during his short reign, Sigismund restored the New Town's former privileges and granted them new ones.

During the interregnum, George of Poděbrady seized control of Prague, penetrating the New Town with his forces from a poorly defended Vyšehrad, and breaking

town hall continued into the reign of the House of Jagellon and culminated in the remodelling of the entire south wing between 1521 and 1526, in which late Gothic architecture and Renaissance elements were interwoven. Furthermore, new Renaissance windows were installed in the corner tower. Restoration work was carried out by Benedict Ried of Pístov. When the large Jewish cemetery in the New Town was closed down in 1478, in the reign of Vladislav II of Jagellon, the area was divided up once again and redeveloped. An example of this work, which has survived to this day, is

The façade of Hlahol House in Prague, an Art Nouveau structure erected on a design by architect Josef Fanta between 1903 and 1905, is adorned with ornamental sculptures by Josef Pekárek

A section of a corner house on Masarykovo nábřeží, richly divided up and embellished by sculptures. This prominent example of the Prague Art Nouveau by Jiří Stibral, with decoration in the same style by Ladislav Šaloun, was erected in 1905 and is located near the National Theatre

through the New Town defences near Karlov and in the Botič valley as well.

As regent of the realm, and later as King of Bohemia, George of Poděbrady looked to the towns for backing, and the New Town supported him to the full. During his regency the New Town inhabitants erected a new, high, prismatic tower onto the town hall, with a gateway running through it. Reconstruction of the

Vladislavova ulice (Vladislav Street). The Šítek Water Tower (Šítkovská vodárenská věž) has stood in its place near the National Theatre and adjacent to Mánes house since 1489. Water was carried from the tower along a wooden conduit and distributed amongst the New Town fountains. In parallel with the erection and renovation of houses for the town-dwellers, construction work on sacred buildings was also being pursued. In

129

The ornate entrance to the Art Nouveau building on Masarykovo nábřeží which formerly housed the Goethe Institute, and which was originally constructed for the Czech Insurance Bank

130

Stucco branches and sculptures of little owls adorn the portal
of a Neo-Gothic Art Nouveau building
on Masarykovo nábřeží

131

The tall nave of a church, towering above the roofs of buildings in the New Town. The church,
on Jungmannovo náměstí (Jungmann Square), is consecrated to Our Lady of the Snows;
Jan Želivský preached here at the beginning of the Hussite Revolution

Vladislav II of Jagellon's reign, a derelict church in Karlov was reconstructed and the vaulting in the sanctuary restored; and attention was devoted to the renovation of the little Church of Our Lady on the Lawn (kostel Panny Marie na Trávníčku), damaged in the siege of Vyšehrad during the Hussite Wars. Construction of the late Gothic freestanding bell tower at the Church of SS Henry and Kunhuta was commenced in the 1470s.

The need to resist pressure from the nobility in their political dispute with it induced the towns to join forces at the beginning of the 16th century. Under Ferdinand I self-government was returned to both towns. The New Town inhabitants participated in the 1547 uprising too, however, and after it failed a number of them were punished, and administration of the town placed under the supervision of a royal magistrate and administrator. Thus the status of the Prague towns, built up over so many years, was destroyed, and the defeat in 1547 condemned them to a passive political rôle.

It was not until the reign of Emperor Rudolf II that economic life began to make a resurgence once again, and it was then that the influences of the innovative Renaissance style of the period began to creep into newly constructed town houses in the New Town as well. In 1609 the Czech Estates held an Assembly at the New Town Hall, and Rudolf finally issued his Imperial Charter on Freedom of Religion. When the town came under threat from forces from Passau, and the New Town showed its readiness to fight, people began attacking monasteries, which they considered to be the root of all. As a consequence, the monastic Church of Our Lady of the Snows and the Karlov monastery incurred serious damage.

The people of the New Town joined the Estates' revolt against the Habsburgs on 23 May 1618. Three of those involved — Valentin Kochan of Prachová, Tobiáš Štefka of Koloděje and Václav Písecký of Granichfeld — were elected to the thirty-member directorate appointed to run the kingdom. Following the defeat inflicted on the Estates' army at White Mountain, many New Town inhabitants paid for their part in the uprising with their lives or their property, or were forced to leave the country. When Swedish armies twice laid siege to Prague during the Thirty Years' War, it became apparent that the New Town fortifications, dating from the mid-14th century, no longer sufficed as a defence against the artillery fire now directed at them, and this led to their being swiftly improved, at least with makeshift elements. Nevertheless, the improvements made to artillery techniques in subsequent years rendered it necessary to erect modern Baroque fortifications.

In the initial stages of renovation in the town after the Treaty of Westphalia brought an end to the Thirty Years' War, the new Baroque style began to make its presence felt, thanks in the main to the construction activities undertaken by the victorious Catholic Church, with the Jesuit Order leading the way, followed by other orders. The Jesuits obtained a large site on which to build in the New Town in the upper part of the cattle market (Karlovo náměstí), and gradually a college complex and Church of St. Ignatius Loyola (kostel sv. Ignáce z Loyoly) came to occupy half of the eastern side of the square. The Church was constructed on a design by Carlo Lurago from 1652 to 1670, and over subsequent decades it was enlarged by other architects (Martin Reiner, Paul Ignaz Bayer) and completed with artistic decoration and furniture. When the Jesuit Order was abolished in 1773, the college became a military hospital.

With regard to sacred architecture, besides being used in the remodelling of the façades and interiors of several older churches, the Baroque style was employed in a number of outstanding structures by the foremost masters of the period. The convent of the Order of St. Elizabeth, found today between the botanical gardens (Botanická zahrada) and Albertov (Albert Quarter), was erected between 1724 and 1732 according to plans drawn up by Kilian Ignaz Dienzenhofer and funded by Margaret Waldstein. A large garden, extending as far as the bottom of the Hill of Winds, belonged to the convent. The members of the Order of St. Elizabeth founded a hospital beside the convent; it was enlarged in the 19th century, and remains in operation today.

Over the site of another church destroyed during the Hussite Wars in the upper New Town, the Augustinians built a new Church of St. Catherine, designed by architect F. M. Kaňka, between 1737 and 1741. This stunning, monolithic Baroque structure has become famed for its magnificent ceiling frescoes by Václav Reiner and stucco work by Giovanni Battista Spinetti.

Between 1699 and 1704 Marco Antonio Canevalle erected a convent church on the corner of present-day Národní třída and Voršilská ulice (Ursula Street).

133

Consecrated to St. Ursula, its façade is graced with sculptures by F. Preiss and J. Kohl. The construction of the convent buildings had been started earlier, in 1674, and was finished in 1722. An equally remarkable structure is the Church of the Holy Trinity (kostel Nejsvětější Trojice), located in Spálená ulice (Burnt Street), adjacent to the Trinitarian monastery. It was founded by Johann Ignaz Putz von Adlerthurn, built on a design by architect Ottavio Broggio, and consecrated in 1703.

A detail from the decoration on the front of the building called The Novaks' (U Nováků) on Vodičkova ulice (Vodička Street). It was erected in 1902 and 1903 on a design by Oswald Polívka, and ranks amongst the most beautiful works of Prague Art Nouveau architecture

In the New Town, as elsewhere, the new Baroque cult of St. John Nepomuk led inevitably to the construction of a new sacred building. The relevant New Town structure is situated south of Karlovo náměstí, above the ancient route leading to Vyšehrad. The Church of St. John Nepomuk on the Rock (kostel sv. Jana Nepomuckého na Skalce), one of the foremost achievements in the architectural work of Kilian Ignaz Dientzenhofer, dates from 1730—1739, and is enhanced by two frontal towers. The Church of St. Carlo Borromeo, with its home for elderly priests, originates from the same period. It now belongs to the Orthodox Church and is consecrated to SS Cyril and Methodius. This impressive work by Dientzenhofer is more recently remembered for its use in harbouring Czech parachutists involved in the assassination attempt on Nazi *Protektor* Reinhard Heydrich in 1942. When the hiding-place was betrayed, the parachutists, rather than fight the superiority of the Nazi forces against the odds, took their own lives.

Many an extraordinary example of the Baroque and Rococo periods may still be seen today in town houses or palace architecture. These styles stand out above all through the decoration and picturesque nature of street house façades, the finishing touches to which were added over the following two centuries in other styles. Let us take a look at a few instances. One of the earlier works by Kilian Ignaz Dientzenhofer is a particularly fascinating summer-house known as Vila Amerika, in the upper part of the New Town, which dates from 1720. The Antonín Dvořák Museum now occupies the palace. Amongst the same architect's last works is the Sylva-Taroucca Palace (palác Sylva-Tarouccovský) on Na Příkopě. Hybernská ulice (Hibernia Street) as it is known today, beginning opposite the Powder Tower and running as far as Masaryk railway station, is home to the early Baroque Kinsky Palace (palác Kinských), dating from 1651 to 1657, designed by the architect Carlo Lurago and commissioned by Johann Anton Losy of Losinthal. The exterior was later remodelled in the Neoclassical style. On the other side of the street stands a second Kinsky Palace, built in around 1700, though all that remains of the original structure after modernisation is the early Baroque portal. The Sweerts-Sporck Palace (palác Sweerts-Sporcků), also situated on Hybernská, ranks amongst the most important palace structures in the New Town. The late Baroque section of the palace, the work of architect Antonín Haffenecker, dates from 1780; the Neoclassical section was added to it a decade later by the architect Palliardi. Ignaz Platzer, a member of the famous Prague family of sculptors, worked on the decoration.

On Panská ulice (Lord Street), between Na Příkopě and Jindřišská ulice (Henry Street), adjacent to the Piarist convent, stand the Baroque Neuberg Palace (palác Neubergovský), erected in about 1730 by J. F. Neus, and the Kaunic Palace (palác Kaunický), the work of architect Giovanni Battista Alliprandi, dating from 1710—1720.

The Enlightenment and Rationalism of the late 18th century influenced the towns' destiny profoundly. Joseph II's abolition of serfdom caused a heavier influx of the rural population into Prague, thereby strengthening its Czech elements. The reforms introduced by his enlightened absolutism paved the way for new ideas. The self-confidence of the middle class, and with it their self-awareness, increased; and parallel to this, national patriotism was gaining ground amongst the aristiocracy, a reaction to the bureaucratic centralism emanating from Vienna. In this favourable climate Neoclassical entered the streets of Prague, becoming the predominant architectural style. It stamped its authority particularly on the New Town, before being replaced by the return of Romanticism linked with ancient forms. The Church of the Holy Cross (kostel sv. Kříže), dating from 1819 to 1824, situated on the corner of Panská ulice and Na Příkopě, is without doubt an interesting example of late Neoclassical, as is the reconstruction work carried out between 1808 and 1811 on the early Baroque

The so-called Šítek Water-Tower (Šítkovská vodárenská věž), was built back in the 15th century, obtained its present likeness as a result of restoration after 1650, and procured its onion dome in the 18th century. The buildings on Masarykovo nábřeží show the styles used in construction in the early 20th century: Neo-Gothic, Neo-Renaissance, Neo-Baroque and Art Nouveau. Jiráskův most (Jirásek Bridge) was constructed between 1929 and 1931

Church of Our Lady, opposite the Powder Tower, now the so-called Hibernian House (dům U Hybernů). The plans for the building work were elaborated by J. Fischer.

Prague began to witness rapid urban development with the advent of industrialisation at the beginning of the 19th century. New industrial suburbs — at first producing textiles, and later housing engineering works — sprang up in places where vineyards, orchards, fields and small villages had once been. Industrialisation affected the New Town only indirectly, however, for though there were still a good many empty or scarcely-occupied plots of land in the New Town, the open spaces outside the walls proved more satisfactory for industry. This left an area suitable for the town's needs, and as a result hospitals, and subsequently university buildings, were constructed in the space between Karlovo náměstí, Karlov and Vyšehrad. A striking example is the complex of plain brick buildings in the style of northern German Gothic architecture, forming the Prague maternity hospital, previously located in the nearby former canon's residence of St. Apollinarius.

The opening of the newly-erected National Theatre, the worthy cultural monument to the Czech nation, in 1881, crowned its and its spiritual representatives' efforts spanning many years. The structure, designed by architect Josef Zítek, who was aided by a multitude of Czech artists, later dubbed the National Theatre Generation, soon burnt down, but after an amazingly short period of two years the theatre reopened in 1883. Painters František Ženíšek, Mikoláš Aleš, Julius Mařák, Vojtěch Hynais and Josef Tulka, and sculptors Bohuslav Schnirch, František Rous, Emanuel Hallmann, Ladislav Šaloun, Antonín Wagner, Jaroslav Štursa and Josef Václav Myslbek, amongst others, undertook the task of decorating the theatre. The ornamentation created for the first time the conditions for combining historical tradition with the contemporary views of Czech society, and was in many respects an act of foundation.

Likewise, the confidence of the national revival movement was stamped on the appearance of the New Town, and of Prague as a whole, in the Neo-Renaissance construction of the National Museum (Národní muzeum) — referred to then as the Muzeum regni Bohemiae — on a design by Josef Schulz. Built at the upper end of Wenceslas Square, it was completed in 1890. However, the origins of this national monument, which became the rock of Czech science and one of the most prominent institutes of collections and sciences in Europe, should be sought in the Institute of Patriots, established by a circle of enthusiastic and educated fine artists and scientists in 1818.

Apart from the most famous Neo-Renaissance structures in Prague New Town — the National Theatre and the National Museum — there exists a large number of other buildings in the same style, typical of the second half of the 19th century. Situated on Na Florenci (Florence Street), where the New Town walls once stood, is the splendid late-18th century Neo-Renaissance Prague Museum, built on the architectural plans of Antonín Wiehl. Collaboration on the rich three-dimensional decoration involved such sculptors and painters as Ladislav Šaloun, Karel Liebschner and Vilém Amort.

A no less fascinating building is that of the former town poorhouse, dating from 1884 and located in Vyšehradská ulice (Vyšehrad Street), which links Karlovo náměstí with Vyšehrad. Allegorical sculptures by Josef Václav Myslbek and Josef Strachovský adorn the vast structure.

It is worth mentioning that not far from there the botanical gardens were established at the end of the 19th century and still exist today, making for an interesting tour. This area of the New Town, lying between Karlovo náměstí and Vyšehrad, houses many Neo-Renaissance buildings containing flats, often with impressive frescoes drawn from themes from Czech history.

The building which occupies the corner of Karlovo náměstí and Resslova ulice (Ressl Street) is a noble example of northern Italian Neo-Renaissance style. The plans for the structure were elaborated by Ignaz Ullmann in 1873, and Josef Václav Myslbek, one of the greatest Czech sculptors, worked on decorating the building as well.

Erected in 1886, the stunning Neo-Renaissance building on Slavonic Island (Slovanský ostrov) opposite the National Theatre still serves its original purpose, namely the hosting of balls, concerts and other events. The island is still also known by its original name, Žofín.

A further example of brilliant Neo-Renaissance architecture is provided by the post office building on Jindřišská, a street off Wenceslas Square. The main hall, with its allegorical frescoes of the postal and courier services, is captivating. The visitor may take

The Baroque summer-house of Václav Michna of Vacínov, known as Amerika,
on ulice Ke Karlovu (Karlov Street), was designed by the
famous architect Kilian Ignaz Dientzenhofer

137

Two New Town churches from the reign of Charles IV. In the Botič river valley,
the small Church of the Annunciation, and on the so-called Hill of Winds
(Větrná hora), the Church of St. Apollinarius (kostel sv. Apolináře)

The Church of Our Lady and Charlemagne (kostel Panny Marie a sv. Karla Velikého)
with the monastery of the Augustinian canons stands at the highest
point of the New Town, above the Botič river valley

139

a look at them whenever he or she likes, for the building performs its original function as Prague's main post office to this day.

The New Town became the focus for Prague's future railway junction from 1845 onwards, when the first train rolled into the town on the newly constructed route taking in Olomouc, Brno and Vienna. The first Prague railway station, built in 1844—1845 and named initially after Emperor Francis I—it is now called Masaryk Station (Masarykovo nádraží) — remains in operation today. The late Neoclassical structure with twin towers was built on a design by Anton Jüngling. The extension of the railway network made it necessary to reconstruct the Prague junction in the 1880s. The new, central Franz Josef I Station — subsequently Wilson Station, and today the Main Station — was built and connected up with all the railway branches, notably after a tunnel was dug under Vinohrady (a Prague district, the name of which means vineyards) for the Budějovice and Linz lines. The station building, dating from 1901—1909, is one of the most precious examples of Prague Art Nouveau architecture which, together with the Neo-Baroque, represents the peak of structural eclecticism and the freedom of forms in the building of modern Prague. The so-called Jubilee Synagogue (Jubilejní synagóga), built in pseudo-Moorish style in 1906 and situated on Jeruzalemská ulice (Jerusalem Street), which links Senovážné náměstí with the area in front of the main railway station, merely confirms the diversity of architectural styles present in the New Town at the turn of the 20th century.

One of the most significant examples of Prague Art Nouveau architecture is the building housing the Prague Hlahol choir on Masarykovo nábřeží (Masaryk Embankment), opposite Slavonic Island. Josef Fanta drew up the plans for the structure, built from 1903 to 1905 and containing stunning sculptures by Josef Pekárek which complement the ornamental decoration of the façade by painter Karel Mottl. Moving a litte way towards the National Theatre one encounters the Goethe Institute standing on a street corner. Architect Jiří Stibral built it in pure Art Nouveau style in 1905, and Ladislav Šaloun provided the rich sculptural decoration. The entire line of façades on the embankment from Jiráskovo náměstí (Jirásek Square) to the National Theatre is an exhibition of the work of Prague's Art Nouveau architects, as well as of fascinating Neo-Gothic, eclectic and Neo-Baroque structures. Yet rather than sitting uncomfortably side by side, the buildings complement one another and give the impression of being part of the same grand architectural design. A definite tourist attraction is the Two Thousand House (dům U Dvou tisíc) — which, like the 1980 house, derives its name from its house number — located on the corner of Jiráskovo náměstí and Rašínovo nábřeží (Rašín Embankment), erected in 1904 on a design by the architect Václav Havel.

The popular restaurant and variety theatre in the house known as The Novaks' (U Nováků) on Vodičkova ulice (Vodička Street), which runs into the middle of Wenceslas Square, are enticing places to visit. As a matter of fact, however, the splendid Art Nouveau building was erected originally for use as a department store, which explains the presence of the allegorical mosaics "Commerce" and "Industry". Another Art Nouveau building, dating from 1906, the Evropa Hotel (originally the Šroubek Hotel) on Wenceslas Square, was designed to cater for the broadest clientele. The hotel boasts a magnificent Art Nouveau façade and a well-preserved interior which remains in use. By contrast, another Art Nouveau hotel, the Hotel Central on Hybernská, is currently out of operation due to large-scale reconstruction. In spite of this, however, the fine Art Nouveau ornamentation employing plant motifs which adorns the building's façade can still be admired.

Wenceslas Square provides a display of exquisite structures dating from the late 19th and early 20th centuries. These include the aforementioned Evropa Hotel from 1906, the 1895 Neo-Baroque palace on the corner of Jindřišská and Wenceslas Square, and the Wiehl House (dům Wiehlův), dating from 1895-1896, on the corner of Vodičkova and Wenceslas Square, its façade graced with genre frescoes in the style of Mikoláš Aleš and Josef Fanta. Furthermore indeed, the perceptive visitor touring the New Town will notice such gems on every square and, moreover, on practically every street.

The New Town has grown more lovely over the years, thankfully by and large escaping unsightly redevelopment, although its status and atmosphere have been severely affecte by the ill-advised placing of a motorway directly through the town centre. In spite of all that, the New Town, with Wenceslas Square at its core, is the busiest and liveliest part of the capital.

Josef Václav Myslbek designed the bronze equestrian figure of St. Wenceslas,
patron saint of the Czech lands, which stands
at the top of Wenceslas Square

141

The door leading into the chapter Church of SS Peter and Paul at Vyšehrad
bears the symbols of the Czech nation — the Czech lion
and the St. Wenceslas eagle

VYŠEHRAD

The bronze sculpture, A Victin of Love and Death, on one of the tombstones at Vyšehrad Cemetery, is the Art Nouveau work of the sculptor Bohumil Kafka

After the example of the ancient Emperor Constantine, King Vratislav carried up twelve panniers on his own shoulders, laid the foundations for the construction, and ordered that a church like the Church of St. Peter in Rome be built at Vyšehrad. In this way, Vratislav, King of Bohemia, through his keen and able mind, humiliated his brother, the Bishop of Prague, for his haughty absence; he chose his church at Vyšehrad to be his final resting place, and enhanced it greatly, both with religious adornments and with its most essential needs and possessions. He appointed the provost of Vyšehrad also chancellor of the realm, and wisely arranged for him to be present at the King's councils and take his seat amongst the foremost men in the kingdom.

IN THE CHRONICLE OF BOHEMIA
BY PŘIBÍK OF RADENÍN, CALLED PULKAVA

143

Legend tells of how on the rugged headland which falls abruptly into the Vltava, the seat of the princes and kings of Bohemia once stood. Vyšehrad was founded in all likelihood some time from the mid-10th century onwards as a second castle for the prince, designed to monitor access to Prague's valley basin from the south. The first authentic testimony of its existence is provided by the denarii struck at the Vyšehrad mint of Boleslav II. In his reign Vyšehrad was the Přemysl fortress, with the prince's palace located on the western side and stone and wooden houses in the centre of the fortifications.

However, castle life really began to flourish in the reign of Prince Vratislav II — or King Vratislav I of Bohemia (1061—1092) — who moved here from Prague Castle. King Vratislav I established at Vyšehrad, amongst other things, a church consecrated to St. Peter, and later also to St. Paul, and established there a chapter independent of the Prague bishopric and subject directly to papal authority. The provost of Vyšehrad held the post of chancellor to the king, as well as to several other rulers. Vratislav also underlined the importance of the alternative royal residence with the construction of a Romanesque stone palace. His Coronation Code most probably dates from 1085. Vyšehrad remained the residence of the Přemysl royal family until the accession of Soběslav I, who decided to transfer the prince's residence back to Prague Castle towards the end of his reign. Thus in the late 12th and 13th centuries Vyšehrad was consigned to second place behind Prague Castle, and for many years the chapter alone used it as its residence.

It was under Charles IV that Vyšehrad regained its political and military importance. He generously allowed remodelling work to be carried out in the modern architectural style of the period, first and foremost on the royal palace. Fully in keeping with the latest military theory and experience, the huge Vyšehrad fortifications were erected between 1348 and 1350. They comprised two main entrance gates, of which Špička, or The Point, a massive transit post on the south side, was still discernible on maps of Prague drawn up in the 16th and 17th centuries. The route from the Prague towns through Vyšehrad and out in the direction of southern Bohemia passed through the second, main gate, known as the Prague Gate or Jerusalem Gate. An important clause in the Code for the Coronation of the Kings of Bohemia issued by Charles IV became the one which stipulated that each future sovereign should make the journey to Vyšehrad on the eve of the coronation ceremony. One might say that Charles laid down the status of the royal castle constitutionally and in legal form, too, by inserting a regulation into the Code which stated that the coronation ceremony should begin at Vyšehrad, which should, in addition, house permantly the bag and bast shoes presumably worn by Přemysl the ploughman when he was called from his work to princess Libuše's throne and became the founder of the first Bohemian dynasty. Charles IV was a descendant of the dynasty on his mother's side, and consistently emphasised his Czech origins.

Reconstruction work on the chapter Church of SS Peter and Paul began after 1369 but was not completed until the next century, despite enjoying royal support from the outset. The model drawn upon for the remodelling was most likely that applied to southern French basilicas. In addition to the prolonged reconstruction of the chapter church, other buildings also underwent renovation, in particular the houses belonging to the dean, canons and other priests. Vyšehrad also received a stone water-supply system in 1361, which provided water from as far afield as the modern-day districts of Pankrác and Jezerka in the Michle area, both a considerable distance away from the Vyšehrad walls by the standards of that period. The entire project was unquestionably connected with the cultivation of grapevines on the southern slopes of the castle headland, and with the need both to irrigate the vines and to provide the inhabitants of Vyšehrad with decent water.

The beginning of the Hussite Revoltion brought Vyšehrad's restored glory to an end. On 1 November 1420 the Vyšehrad garrison loyal to Sigismund of Luxemburg, King of Hungary and Rome, starved by a long siege, surrendered the castle to the allied Hussite armies. The reason for this was that on the same day the successor to the throne of Bohemia, whom the Hussites had not recognised, was routed on a plain at Pankrác by the citizens of Prague and their Hussite allies from Tábor, Žatec, Louny, Slaný and the Union of Oreb from, eastern Bohemia, before the eyes of the inhabitants of Vyšehrad, whom he wished to rescue from the siege with his own forces. The Vyšehrad mercenaries were gallant in their respect for the conditions of

The large-scale building work undertaken in the reign of Charles IV also affected Vyšehrad. The monarch devoted much attention to the most important place connected with the tradition surrounding the Přemysl dynasty; Charles was a descendant of that dynasty on his mother's side

A vista through the Wiehl arcades at Vyšehrad Cemetery. Rudolf Říhovský worked on the painted Neo-Renaissance decoration

An example of decoration on a tombstone at Vyšehrad Cemetery. The round sculpted portrait is by Josef Václav Myslbek

Žal (Grief), a statue by František Bílek, a master of Czech symbolism, on the grave of writer Václav Beneš Třebízský

The origin of these three unusual stone colums is the subject
of much speculation. One legend refers to them
as the Devil's stones

147

the armistice declared with the Hussites some days earlier, and did not intervene during the battle. In the aftermath, the Vyšehrad fortifications were pulled down in a number of places opposite the town and the abandoned castle complex joined up with the New Town. An attempt was made in the late 1400s, during the reign of Vladislav II of Jagellon, to establish the town of Vyšehrad Hill, but the community, comprising predominantly small craftsmen, merely eked out a living here for a century and a half, in particular after the property rights of the Vyšehrad chapter were restored in the 16th century.

In the light of a decision taken by Ferdinand III, from 1654 Vyšehrad began its transformation into a massive Baroque citadel as part of the reconstruction of the Prague fortifications which had proved so antiquated and frail under assault from Swedish artillery during the Thirty Years' War. This merely reconfirmed the key rôle then enjoyed by Vyšehrad as a fortress guarding access to Prague from the south and southeast in military operations directed at the town. The defence system of the Baroque fortress was established on a basic pentagonal outline surrounded by brick walls with robust corner bastions. The entire project benefited from the Italian and Dutch schools' sound experience of military fortifications, the plans used in their construction having been drawn up by Inocence Conti and Giuseppe Priami. Until the fortress was abolished in 1866, only the chapter at the Church of SS Peter and Paul survived there in its original capacity.

In 1883 Vyšehrad and the community below it were elevated to the rank of sixth municipal district, though the citadel was administered by the military until 1911.

Once the stronghold had been discontinued as such, the patriotic canons played a considerable rôle in restoring Vyšehrad to its traditional glory, this time as a national cultural monument. The little Vyšehrad Cemetery (Vyšehradský hřbitov) became the place in which the leading figures in the national revival, political life and culture of the 19th century were laid to rest, and since that time it has remained the national cemetery of greatest importance. The fortress area was later redeveloped into a public park. Even today the utmost care is devoted to Vyšehrad, and it is the subject of systematic architectural research insofar as the complex surface and structural conditions permit. The

oldest surviving monument at Vyšehrad, recalling its growth under King Vratislav, is the Romanesque rotunda of St. Martin (rotunda sv. Martina). The 11th-century structure stands near the Leopold Gate (Leopoldova brána), the second interior gate of the Baroque fortress, dating from 1676—1678.

The early Romanesque basilica of SS Peter and Paul, founded in the late 11th century, had already been greatly enlarged by the early 12th century, and was remodelled in early Gothic style in the second half of the 13th century. The church was completely rebuilt and splendidly decorated under Charles IV, but when Vyšehrad fell in 1420 it incurred serious damage. Following the return of the chapter, the structure underwent renovation once again in the 16th and early 17th centuries, and in the first half of the 18th century the creators of the Prague Baroque, František Maximilián Kaňka, Giacomo Antonio Canevalle and Giovanni Santini worked to various extents on alterations to the church. Its current appearance is the result of rebuilding in Neo-Gothic style in the late 19th century, overseen by Josef Mocker. High Neo-Gothic twin towers designed by František Mikš were constructed in 1902—1903. A striking feature is the tympanum on the main portal with a relief of the Last Judgment from 1901, as are the ornate Art Nouveau ornamental frescoes inside the church.

The Vyšehrad Cemetery was founded at the initiative of provost Václav Stulc on the site of the former parish graveyard. Leading architects Antonín Barvitius, Antonín Wiehl and Josef Sakař worked on adaptations to the complex. The most celebrated personalities in 19th- and 20th-century Czech artistic, scientific and political life are buried in the cemetery, the dominant feature of which is the pantheon, or slavín, a massive crypt built in 1889—1890 by the architect Antonín Wiehl and decorated by Josef Mauder. Here one may find the graves of a good many personalities, often famous also throughout Europe, and even the world, as well as numerous works of funeral architecture and the plastic arts. The cemetery is considered to be a unique, architecturally well-balanced entity, a memorial both to Czech history and to the present day.

As seen from the corner of the fortress above the Vyšehrad rock, the view of Prague Castle, the Vltava and its bridges is one the visitor to Vyšehrad will never forget.

From the Lesser Quarter side of the Vltava river one is afforded a view of the Charles Bridge and the Old Town Bridge Tower, a Gothic structure built by Peter Parler in the latter half of the 14th century

A view from a tower on St. Vitus' Cathedral, looking out onto the castle complex, includes the twin white towers of the Church of St. George (kostel sv. Jiří), and beyond them the Black Tower (Černá věž). Both serve as reminders of the Romanesque period at Prague Castle

PRAGUE
AN HISTORIC TOWN

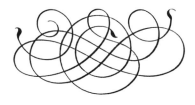

MARIE VITOCHOVÁ

JINDŘICH KEJŘ

JIŘÍ VŠETEČKA

Cover, binding and typographical layout by Václav Rytina

Translation into English by Mark Prescott, BA, Second edition, Prague, 1994
Published by V RÁJI Publishing House (V Ráji 229, Prague 9), 24th edition,
152 pages, 121 colour photographs
Editors in chief Marie Vitochová and Jindřich Kejř
Printed by Pardubice, Printing House (Smilova 487, Pardubice)